JEWISH COOKING BOOT CAMP

THE MODERN GIRL'S GUIDE TO COOKING LIKE A JEWISH GRANDMOTHER

WITHDRAWN

ThreeForks

GUILFORD, CONNECTICUT
HELENA, MONTANA
AN IMPRINT OF
GLOBE PEQUOT PRESS

ANDREA MARKS CARNEIRO & ROZ MARKS

FOR OUR TWO EDIES

To buy books in quantity for corporate use
or incentives, call **(800) 962–0973**
or e-mail **premiums@GlobePequot.com.**

ThreeForks®

Three Forks® is an imprint of The Globe Pequot Press.

Illustrations: Georgiana Goodwin © Morris Book Publishing, LLC
Text design: Georgiana Goodwin
Project editors: Julie Marsh, Jennifer Taber

Library of Congress Cataloging-in-Publication Data is available on file.
ISBN 978-0-7627-5088-7

Printed in the United States of America

10 9 8 7 6 5 4 3 2 1

CONTENTS

Foreword   v

Acknowledgments   vii

Introduction   viii

The Basics   1

Shabbat   15

Rosh Hashanah   29

Yom Kippur   45

Break the Fast   57

Chanukah   69

Passover   95

A Few More Jewish Holidays   127

Take-Along Foods   135

Comfort Foods   153

Metric Conversion Tables   180

Index   181

About the Authors   190

FOREWORD

L'or v d'or

One of the most vivid and cherished childhood memories I hold centers around our visits with Grandma Rose in Rockaway Beach, New York. Several times a year my dad, mom, sister, and I would drive from our home in Bethesda, Maryland, to Grandma Rose and Grandpa Lou's place on Long Island. Their walkup was small and cluttered, but the central room for me was the tiny kitchen. I will always remember the distinct smells, familiar tastes, gregarious chatter, and simple joy of sitting, for hours it seemed, at their crowded kitchen table while Grandma Rose showered us with an overabundance of delicious, homemade Jewish foods.

From her perspective, she could never make enough for us nor could we consume enough of what she made. From my perspective, I felt her steady love and adoration for my dad, extended now to his family, expressed through her caring preparation and presentation of Jewish foods for us. As I look back, I think the consistency, generosity, and pleasure of her creating family memories through food has deeply shaped me.

Today, I spend less and less time in my own kitchen as I work on issues of social justice and gender equity that often take me far from home. Yet, I regularly return to my kitchen for grounding. For it is at our kitchen and dining tables, often imbued with food prepared with my Grandma Rose's recipes (captured by the diligent measuring and surveillance of my Aunt Bea who shadowed my grandma years ago), that I too seek to transmit the message of my relentless love for our growing family and my deep craving to nurture and gather my family to create memories that will sustain us now and inspire the next generations.

Grandma Rose taught me how to actualize the fundamental Jewish value of *l'or v d'or*— passing values, traditions, and dreams from generation to generation. I try to do it in many ways, perhaps the most delicious of which is through food.

—NANCY RATZAN

Nancy is a lawyer and a social justice activist. She is currently the national president of the National Council of Jewish Women and a national leader who works to ensure powerful grassroots engagement in progressive social issues. Her husband, Kenneth, and their blended family of three daughters, three sons, two daughters-in-law, and four grandchildren enjoy the gathering of family, always marked by wonderful food.

ACKNOWLEDGMENTS

Thank you to all the friends and family who gave us support and encouragement as we worked to make *Jewish Cooking Boot Camp* a reality.

To Ellen Cohen and Jill Kaplan, the original Boot Campers and unofficial Marks family members. Their love of latkes sparked 200 pages.

To Adina Kahn for believing in our concept and to Jane Dystel for being our advocate and adviser.

To our wonderful editor Heather Carriero for bringing our vision to life and to Julie Marsh and the rest of the team at GPP for their hard work.

To everyone who donated their family recipes and traditions to make this book so complete.

And most of all to David, Sarah, Jacob, Gil, Edie, and Allan for their love, their ideas, and most of all . . . their appetites.

INTRODUCTION

The idea for *Jewish Cooking Boot Camp* started a long, long, long time ago. You see, when you live in New York but your parents live in Miami . . . well, they end up with a lot of house-guests. In my case those guests were a small group of my friends who spent every winter holiday (and some others) flying down to bask in the sun and fun of Miami. We would take over my parents' house with our suitcases and winter coats, spend all night running around South Beach, and finally end up gathered in the kitchen the next morning to share our stories from New York City with my parents as we picked over the seemingly unlimited food my mom, Roz, would have waiting.

As the years passed I eventually left New York, but my friends kept up their commute to Miami. We got new jobs and new apartments and new boyfriends, but our jet-set visits never changed. The annual Marks family Chanukah party raged on, and Roz's latkes continued their steady climb to legend status. One holiday, as we sat around the kitchen, my friend Ellen suddenly had a realization. "What happens," she asked, "when we all have our own families and we have to start cooking for ourselves?" We were silent. And an idea was born.

At first it was a joke. We envisioned a long weekend, a syllabus, a holiday-by-holiday game plan designed to teach us everything from brisket to kasha and *varnishkas,* cabbage soup to nut cake. We laughed and moved on. But soon I realized that a Jewish Cooking Boot Camp was, in fact, an amazing idea. I thought of the millions of young people out there who were looking for guidance but were too intimidated to pick up a traditional cookbook, or who had grandmothers and mothers (like mine) who cooked without recipes, or who simply didn't have the time to learn in a traditional setting. I thought of my mom and how she defied the stereotype of a traditional Jewish cook. She was young and cool and had a career. She could just as easily navigate her way around a good Neiman's sale as she could a noodle kugel. She made Jewish cooking less intimidating.

The truth is this: It's incredibly difficult to become a great chef, but it's very simple to cook dinner for your family. My mom always says that if you have good recipes, you're two-thirds of the way there. And that's what we're giving you.

What we have put together is a compilation of recipes gathered over centuries. From the cardboard box stowed on top of my mom's fridge, we have sifted through scraps of paper, scribbled notes, and old e-mails and letters. Some of the recipes come from my aunt, grandmother, and great-grandmother; some come from great-aunts, cousins, and distant relatives; some come from friends or friends-of-friends; and some . . . well, some we have no idea where they came from. But they're good.

This book isn't about keeping kosher or following rules. The recipes we've included are good old traditional holiday favorites that always seem to please. Each chapter provides a little background (and a little fun) for those interested, as well as some inspiration in the form of real-world traditions from families around the globe. We have also provided you (courtesy of the wonderful Michael Bittel, owner of Sunset Corners Fine Wines & Spirits in Miami, Florida) with wine suggestions for each holiday menu—a moderately priced red and white (under $12) and a special-occasion red and white (up to $20). All of the wines are nationally distributed and easily available at most liquor stores, wine shops, and in some cases, grocery stores.

We hope the recipes inspire you to host your own family holidays . . . to pull out (or go buy) a beautiful tablecloth and wine glasses and good china, and to light candles and sing songs and serve up ridiculous amounts of food that no one could possibly ever finish. Because once you do, we're sure that those feelings of pride and love and excitement will fill you with so much joy that your holidays will never be the same again.

—ANDREA MARKS CARNEIRO

THE BASICS

"My grandmother was a Jewish juggler: she used to worry about six things at once."

—RICHARD LEWIS

If the thought of entertaining a large group of people causes a panic attack, we're here to tell you that you're not alone. Even the most seasoned chef has gone cold when faced with entertaining guests in the double-digit range (not to mention a mob of hungry family members). The only difference is experience. Once you make it through your first holiday, the fear will subside. We're not going to lie; it's stressful and it's overwhelming, but the sense of pride you'll feel when it's over is worth every pressed napkin and every second batch. To that end we've put together a cheat sheet of some basics to help you navigate the choppy waters of holiday entertaining.

THE LIST (PART 1)

Holidays are unpredictable. No matter how hard you try, there will always be a last-minute jolt to your well-laid plans. Whether it's your suddenly vegetarian sister or surprise cousins from out of town, you can fend off disaster by keeping your pantry, refrigerator, and freezer stocked with these holiday essentials:

A 12- to 16-ounce bag of egg noodles (medium size)

All-purpose flour, presifted, bleached or unbleached

Boxes of vanilla and orange cake mixes (a great base for desserts)

Boxes of vanilla pudding (to add into the cake mix)

Brown sugar (light or dark)

Chicken broth/beef broth

12-ounce bag of semi-sweet chocolate chips

Coffee and tea

Confectioners' sugar (powdered sugar)

Cooking spray and baking spray (baking spray, such as Baker's Joy, has flour in it)

Cottage cheese
Dozen extra-large eggs (always use extra-large eggs when cooking)
Extra chicken breasts and a whole chicken
Fat-free sour cream
Frozen vegetables (spinach and broccoli are always easy go-tos and simple to dress up)
Garlic
Knorr's vegetable soup mix (a great base for a quick veggie dip)
Kosher salt
Mayonnaise
Onions (preferably Vidalia onions as they are sweet and mild)
Potatoes
Pound of margarine and/or butter—both come salted and unsalted (and keep for months in the freezer)
Pound of sweet unsalted butter (keeps for months in the freezer)
Red and white wines
Sugar
Vanilla extract

MENU-PLANNING TIPS

- Write out your menu in advance and make a list of all the ingredients needed to check off as you buy them.
- For more than eight people, serve a minimum of two or three appetizers.
- Figure on about ½ pound of beef per person and at least one piece of chicken as well.
- Always, always serve salad and at least one plain vegetable for the picky eaters.
- When buying a brisket, look for a "first cut"; it will be leaner (see our brisket buying guide in the Rosh Hashanah chapter).
- For the dessert course, you can never go wrong in offering fresh fruit alongside any sweeter options.

PREPARING FOR GUESTS

- Anything that can be made beforehand should be.
- If you can't fit all your guests at one table, you may want to do a buffet. It will keep the table tops less crowded and prevent you from running back and forth all night.
- A few days beforehand, set out all your serving pieces and place Post-It notes inside each one indicating what dish will go where. That way if you're missing any pieces, you have time to buy or borrow.
- Set your table ahead of time! Give yourself time to make sure tablecloths and napkins are cleaned and pressed.
- Speaking of which . . . a tablecloth makes any holiday a little more special, as do cloth napkins and good silver. (No paper plates!)
- For easy decor, stick to fresh flowers and candles—just beware of anything scented.

BASIC KITCHEN CONVERSIONS

1 tablespoon = 3 teaspoons	⅜ cup = 6 tablespoons	8 fluid ounces = 1 cup
¹⁄₁₆ cup = 1 tablespoon	½ cup = 8 tablespoons	1 pint = 2 cups
⅛ cup = 2 tablespoons	⅔ cup = 10 tablespoons + 2 teaspoons	1 quart = 2 pints
⅙ cup = 2 tablespoons + 2 teaspoons	¾ cup = 12 tablespoons	4 cups = 1 quart
¼ cup = 4 tablespoons	1 cup = 48 teaspoons	1 gallon = 4 quarts
⅓ cup = 5 tablespoons + 1 teaspoon	1 cup = 16 tablespoons	16 ounces = 1 pound

THE LIST (PART 2)

We know your kitchen may not look like the inside of a Williams-Sonoma catalog, but there are a few basics that every cook should own when embarking on holiday preparation. Many of the items below can be purchased in the grocery store. However, it is always money well spent to buy quality pots and pans, as well as a good food processor and stand mixer. Every kitchen should be stocked with the following:

1½- or 2-quart casserole dish

1 cupcake/muffin pan

1 garlic press

1 small silicone spatula for baking

1 stainless-steel spatula

10-inch Bundt pan

12-inch frying pan with lid

2 baking sheets (1 regular baking sheet and 1 jellyroll baking sheet, a baking sheet with sides)

2 9-inch cake pans

2 good wine openers (it never hurts to have a backup!)

2-quart pot (sauces, vegetables)

6- or 8-quart pot (soups, pastas)

8-inch pan

9–12-inch springform pan

9 x 13-inch glass baking dish

Food processor

Hand beater

Stand mixer (I love my Mixmaster and wouldn't try any other kind!)

ANDREA'S TIPS

Having lived in tiny New York apartments for most of my post-college life, I didn't really begin to experiment in the kitchen until I moved back to Miami and had the time (and space) to truly cook. In those past six years, I learned a lot of lessons the hard way. Here are a few of my best general tips for the kitchen:

Organize Your Ingredients

You can make life a lot easier by gathering everything you need and setting it on the counter before you start. You'll quickly see if you're missing something, and you won't be distracted trying to find things. (There is nothing worse than getting halfway through a recipe and realizing that you are missing a key ingredient.) Then, as you use each ingredient, put it away. It will save you time and space.

Preparation Is Key

Read the recipe all the way through before starting; it will help you manage your time and keep you on track. If you have to use spices or extracts, take the tops or lids off early on—before your hands become covered in flour or oil. And don't forget to preheat the oven if need be; it can take a while and can set you back if you forget.

Clean as You Go

Don't wait until the end to clean up. If you spill a little flour, wipe it up. If you use a measuring cup, wash it or stick it in the dishwasher. Wash out pots or pans while things are heating up on the stove. In small kitchens there is nothing worse than a pile of dirty dishes waiting for you.

Know Your Kitchen

Every oven and burner is different. Some are hotter and need less time, and some are the opposite. Pay attention to how recipes come out and adjust accordingly. My oven gets incredibly hot, so I often have to shave a few minutes off cooking times, where my mom's oven often needs more time to compensate for less heat. Even the little things can make a difference.

In one house my burners weren't quite level, and I would have to prop up the end of the pan to make sure my food cooked evenly. A small price to pay for a big difference in taste!

Be Safe
I am a total klutz in the kitchen. I have sliced and diced my fingers more times than I can count, burned fingers and arms reaching into ovens, and once almost burned down the kitchen as a result of a stray candle meeting some floaty curtains. As a result (and upon the insistence of my husband), I always keep my cabinet stocked with hydrogen peroxide, band-aids, baking soda, and a mini fire extinguisher.

TWO FAIL-SAFE CROWD-PLEASERS

Even if your main course falls short (it happens), you can never go wrong with a great starter and a great dessert. A vegetable basket curbs hunger and generally pleases even the pickiest of noshers, and a beautiful fruit salad to end the meal adds color and vibrancy to the table while complementing almost any sweet offering. Always include the vegetable basket as one of your appetizers and a fruit as one of your desserts

The Burning Question: Everything You Ever Wanted to Know about Kitchen Injuries

(Courtesy of Dr. Ronaldo Carneiro, M.D.—hand surgeon and mandelbrot fanatic)

- The most important tip is that when slicing anything (veggies, fruit, potatoes, etc.), make sure you use a cutting board and slice with the blade toward the board—do not try to slice any food item in your hand.
- Always be careful when removing knives from the dishwasher. If possible, place knives in the dishwasher blade-first.
- Throw away dull knives—they are more dangerous than knives that cut well.
- Never stick your hand inside a food processor, garbage disposal, or blender while it is still on. (This seems kind of obvious, but many of my patients incur injuries that way.)
- For minor cuts: Hold the wound under water for 2 minutes. If it continues bleeding, hydrogen peroxide is good; otherwise water is the best way to clean the wound.
- Pressure is the best way to stop the bleeding of a deep cut. Any artery or vein that is cut will eventually stop bleeding with sufficient direct pressure. One thing that is not advised is applying a tourniquet to the bleeding limb, often seen in movies. For that to be effective, one has to make it so tight that the arterial circulation stops. It can be a dangerous maneuver if tried by a person without adequate training.
- For minor burns: Apply ice for 5 to 10 minutes right away—it stops the burn from intensifying. Burns can spread on the surface as well as in depth. Ice will prevent both.
- If you have an accident and slice off a piece of your finger, place the detached piece in a plastic bag, then in a cooler with ice, and bring it to the emergency room. This gives your best chance of reattachment. Do not place it directly on ice or in water or another substance.
- A doctor should look at any injuries that continue bleeding after all the above measures are taken for about 10 minutes without success. Also, call a doctor for any injuries that cause loss of sensation or motion of the injured body part. Deformities at or close to a knuckle can also represent fractures and dislocations that should be seen by a qualified physician.

VEGETABLE BASKET

A vegetable basket is the perfect appetizer for any dinner or holiday meal. It also makes a beautiful centerpiece. Follow these simple directions.

SERVES: 10–12   PREPARATION TIME: 45–55 MINUTES

Head of romaine lettuce
2–2½-pound head of cabbage with large green leaves
1 16-ounce package precut carrot sticks (or cut them up yourself)
1 10-ounce package precut cauliflower florets, ends snipped off
1 16-ounce package precut celery sticks (or cut them up yourself)
1 8-ounce package radishes, ends snipped off
1 10-ounce package precut broccoli florets, ends snipped off
2 yellow peppers, cut in strips
2 medium cucumbers, peeled and sliced

1. Use a round basket approximately 14 x 14 inches and no more than 5 to 6 inches in depth. Crinkle up pieces of newspaper and fill in the bottom of the basket so that the newspaper is even with the top of the basket. Cover the newspaper with waxed paper.
2. Pull the leaves off the romaine lettuce carefully and rinse them with cold water. Place the lettuce leaves over the waxed paper horizontally, going around the basket and pushing down on the waxed paper. Make sure the leaves overlap each other and the edge of the basket.
3. Carefully pull the large green leaves off the head of cabbage. You are going to use the cabbage to create a "bowl" to hold your dip. You will need about 6 leaves, depending on how big they are.
4. Once you have taken the large leaves off, slice about ½ inch off the bottom of the cabbage so it is flat and will not roll. Also slice about 1¼ inch off the top of the cabbage, over the core. After trimming the top of the cabbage, start in the middle and carve a hole—keep digging out the cabbage a little at a time until you have what looks like a bowl.

5. Once you have a bowl, take the large cabbage leaves and put them around the bowl like flower petals. Place the bowl in the center of the basket with the leaves hugging around it (it should look like a closed-up flower).
6. Place the carrot sticks horizontally in one pile next to the bowl, then pile the cauliflower florets next to the carrots, and continue around the cabbage bowl with the other vegetables in the following order: celery, radishes, broccoli, yellow pepper strips, and cucumber slices. You probably will not use all the vegetables at first, but keep them in the refrigerator to refill the veggie basket. Trust us, it goes quickly.

✳ You can make the basket in the morning and cover it with wet paper towels to keep the vegetables crisp all day. You will need to re-dampen the towels every couple of hours or so.

SPiNACH DiP

As far as dips go, this is our favorite. It's easy, looks nice, works well for any occasion, and we have yet to meet someone who didn't like it!

SERVES: 8   PREPARATION TIME: 15 MINUTES
REFRIGERATE FOR AT LEAST 3 HOURS (BEST IF IT SITS OVERNIGHT)

1 package Knorr vegetable soup mix
16 ounces fat-free sour cream
1 cup mayonnaise
1 package frozen chopped spinach, thawed and squeezed dry

Combine all of the ingredients and mix well. When ready to serve, spoon the dip into the "cabbage bowl" you made for the Vegetable Basket or another pretty bowl.

✳ Make sure the spinach is well dried; if it's still watery it will make the dip watery as well.

AVOCADO-TOMATO DIP

An alternative dip, for those who don't like spinach, is this tangy sour cream–based vegetable dip, which is also quite easy.

SERVES: 10   PREPARATION TIME: 10 MINUTES
REFRIGERATE FOR AT LEAST 2–3 HOURS

16 ounces fat-free sour cream
2 packages dry Italian dressing mix
2 tablespoons mayonnaise
2 teaspoons lemon juice
1 medium avocado, peeled and chopped fine
1 medium tomato, peeled and chopped
¼ teaspoon Tabasco sauce or to taste (optional)

1. Put all of the above ingredients into a food processor or blender and mix until smooth.
2. Chill for 2 to 3 hours. When ready to serve, spoon the dip into the "cabbage bowl."

✳ A ripe avocado is dark green and semisoft to the touch.

FRESH FRUIT

*Roz's son (and Andrea's brother) David is the child who has truly mastered this dessert.
Imagine our surprise when we arrived at his home for a birthday party to find a fully sculpted
watermelon basket filled with a beautiful fruit salad (he used a melon baller).
Even his wife was impressed . . .*

SERVES: 8   PREPARATION TIME: 10 MINUTES

¼ seedless watermelon
2 cantaloupes
1 honeydew melon
1 pound red seedless grapes
1 pineapple
1 pint strawberries

Cut all the fruit into bite-sized pieces. Layer one fruit at a time in a clear bowl, or just mix it all together.

* It looks prettier when layered one fruit at a time. Place in this order: watermelon, cantaloupe, honeydew, red grapes, pineapple, and strawberries

* You can also serve just one fruit for dessert. For example, cut up one or two pineapples and serve pineapple slices on a platter, or serve a large bowl of seedless red and green grapes. A large bowl of fresh strawberries is another option.

Once and for All: Leftovers

Ahhhh . . . the day after. When the guests are gone and the chatting has quieted. When the dishes are clean and the oven is off. When the fridge is still . . . overflowing with food? It's the age-old question: What to do with leftovers? We asked our good friend Chef Michael B. Jacobs, owner of MediterAsia Consulting, Inc., in Miami Beach, Florida, for the answer. Here are his suggestions:

Challah Stuffing

Cook down some celery, onion, and carrots along with garlic and a bouillon cube. Add some challah and white wine and mix together with whatever seasonings you like (garlic powder, onion powder, bay leaf, thyme). Add some chicken stock and place in an ovenproof pan. Cover and cook at 350°F for 15 to 20 minutes, removing the lid for the last 10 minutes.

Whitefish Dip

Take your leftover whitefish and mix with a little sour cream, mayo, and horseradish. Serve with bagel chips for a great snack or appetizer.

Brisket Paninis

Shred your leftover brisket with a little of the jus. Place on ciabatta bread with lettuce and tomato, or throw in some pickles (or leftover horseradish) to add a little kick.

Matzo Bread Crumbs

Throw your leftover matzo into a food processor with a little bit of seasoning, and voilà! Instant bread crumbs. Use them as a batter for chicken or add them to turkey burgers or meatballs.

Chicken Stew

Shred your leftover roasted chicken into a saucepan of carrots, onion, celery, and chicken broth. Reduce it down and add leftover roasted potatoes.

Fajitas

Heat your leftover flank steak (or chicken) and asparagus along with store-bought tortillas. Puree your leftover spinach with a little sour cream, lemon juice, and cilantro for a quick topping, or chop some onions, tomatoes, and asparagus for a light salsa.

SHABBAT

"If you don't put in the effort the day before, what are you going to eat on Shabbat?"

—TALMUD AVODAH ZARAH 3A

Whether orthodox or reform, preparation is always key when it comes to Shabbat. Capping off a busy week with a family dinner is a great idea, but spending all day Friday in a kitchen isn't always feasible. For that reason we've given you dishes that are simple to make, many of which can be prepared during the week. The appetizers, onion kugel, salad dressing, and ice cream pie can all be made in advance, leaving plenty of time on Friday to prep and cook the chicken. Another benefit? Having many elements of the menu finished in advance creates fewer pots and pans to clean after dinner! And when it comes to baking the challah, just remember one thing: Homemade is lovely on special occasions, but there's no shame in bakery-bought bread. In fact, a local temple or school is likely to sell fresh challah on Friday as a fundraiser.

WINE SUGGESTIONS

Moderately Priced Red:
Monte Antico (Tuscany, Italy)

Special-Occasion Red:
Braida Monte Bruna Barbera (Piedmont, Italy)

Moderately Priced White:
Bernier Chardonnay (Loire, France)

Special-Occasion White:
Cambia Katherines Vineyard Chardonnay (Santa Barbara, California)

REAL WORLD TRADITIONS

"At our Shabbat dinner we go around the table and share our highs (best part of our week) and our lows (worst part of our week), and then we each say what we are looking forward to in the coming week. It's a really nice way for our kids to learn how to speak in front of a group (even though it is usually just the five of us—we do this even when we have company or are out to eat), and it is also a great way for them to learn how to listen to one another and to see that their parents also have bad days sometimes! We do our 'highs and lows' after the Shabbat blessings, and then after dinner we sing Shabbat songs and either play board games or take a walk. We try to do this as many Friday nights as possible."

—WENDY, PHILADELPHIA, PENNSYLVANIA

"I bring my twin girls home early from school on Fridays so that we can bake together for Shabbat. We make challah, and we also bake a dessert for Shabbat dinner. On Friday morning before school I give the girls cookbooks with pictures, since they cannot read yet, to pick out what dessert they want. While they are in school, I go shopping for ingredients. They love placing the ingredients into the mixer and making sure all the right ingredients go into the recipe. They also love to knead the dough for the challah. They show such pride at Shabbat dinner that they have made the dessert and challah. I love that at least once a week I get to spend true quality time with my girls."

—AVISHAG, NORTH MIAMI, FLORIDA

"Every Friday morning I wake up at 6 a.m. and begin to prepare Shabbat dinner for at least eight and sometimes up to fourteen people. This is a new tradition for my husband and me, who only began seriously observing the Sabbath once our son was born. No matter what is happening with work or how many endless business and social obligations we need to attend, Friday night is sacred. We do not go out, we don't get in a car or on a plane, and our BlackBerries, cells, and computers are all off. It's just us and whomever we decide to invite into our home. The whole world gets shut out, we say kiddush and the other blessings, and the fun begins.

"We have lots of non-Jewish friends and invite them to Shabbat dinner along with our Jewish friends. We always try to explain what is going on in funny, non-boring ways. For example, after the kiddush I usually say, 'This means, thank God we have wine!' We also usually end up playing 'Rock Band' on the Playstation afterward, unless our guests are *shomer* shabbat, in which case, we keep drinking and chatting for the rest of the night. They stumble home, and we pray we don't break any of our china or crystal.

"The question I get most often is: How did you pull this off and make it look so easy? It's a long complicated answer that involves a nanny, a kosher butcher that delivers, and frantic calls to my husband that he needs to be home by 6 p.m. sharp. There is a lot of hard work involved to pull this off, and sometimes I wonder why I am doing this to myself. Okay, every Friday by midday I get there! But it is worth it every time in the end."

—DEB, NEW YORK CITY, NEW YORK

THE FACTS

1. Shabbat begins at sunset, but the Shabbat candles that welcome the Sabbath are traditionally lit eighteen minutes before sundown.
2. Many believe Shabbat to be the most important holy day in the Jewish calendar, and it is often referred to as a "queen" or "bride."
3. *Hachnasat orchim* (or hosting guests) is considered a mitzvah in the Jewish religion and is especially encouraged for Shabbat meals.

DID YOU KNOW?

- Shabbat is the only ritual observance instituted in the Ten Commandments.
- The two candles lit on Shabbat represent the two commandments of Shabbat: *zakhor* (remember) and *shamor* (observe).
- While the woman of the house welcomes Shabbat by saying the prayer over the candles, the man of the house says the prayer over the wine (see Shabbat Blessings on page 28).
- Shabbat is considered officially over on Saturday night when one can count three stars in the sky.
- Sex is not only encouraged between spouses on Shabbat, it is actually considered a double mitzvah!

SPiNACH CHEESE SQUARES

These cheese squares are such an old recipe that no one in our family can remember who passed it along. Though they may be small, they pack a lot of spinach flavor; when we tested them at a weeknight family dinner, they disappeared before we could even ask if anyone liked them.

SERVES: 10–12   PREPARATION TIME: 15 MINUTES
COOKING TIME: 35 MINUTES (PLUS 40–50 MINUTES OF COOLING TIME)

2 tablespoons butter or margarine
2 eggs
½ cup flour
½ cup milk
½ teaspoon salt
½ teaspoon baking powder
8 ounces Monterey Jack cheese, grated (or any packaged blend of shredded Monterey Jack)
1 8-ounce package chopped spinach, thawed and drained

1. Preheat the oven to 350°F.
2. Melt the butter and pour it into an 8 x 11-inch baking dish.
3. In a large bowl beat the eggs; add the flour, milk, salt, and baking powder. Mix well.
4. Add the cheese and spinach. Mix well.
5. Pour the mixture into the baking dish.
6. Bake for 35 minutes—or until set and golden brown on top.
7. Let cool for 40 to 50 minutes. Cut into bite-sized squares and serve.

* Whenever you work with frozen chopped spinach, be sure to drain it well. If you don't have time to let it sit in a colander for a few hours, paper towels can work well to squeeze out excess water.

* These squares are easily prepared in advance and reheated prior to serving (or the next day).

GRANDMA EDITH'S ONION NOODLE KUGEL

Full disclosure: Andrea hates sweets. And raisins. So her loving Grandma Edith would always make this favorite for her at family holidays. It takes the sweet flavor out of kugel and replaces it with a more savory taste that works well with the garlic flavor of the chicken. Call it a different take on a Jewish classic.

SERVES: 12 · PREPARATION TIME: 20 MINUTES
COOKING TIME: 50–60 MINUTES

12-ounce package egg noodles, cooked per instructions on package
1 stick butter (or margarine), melted
16 ounces low-fat small-curd cottage cheese
4 eggs
¼ small onion, grated
½ teaspoon salt
¼ teaspoon pepper

1. Preheat the oven to 350°F.
2. Mix all ingredients in a large bowl and season with salt and pepper to taste.
3. Pour the mixture into a 9 x 13 x 2-inch baking dish, greased with butter or cooking spray.
4. Dot the top with a little extra butter.
5. Bake for 60 minutes or until golden brown on top.
6. Salt to taste right before serving.

The Thirty-nine Categories of Forbidden Acts on Shabbat

The thirty-nine forbidden acts (or thirty-nine *melachot*) form the basic outline of activities that are forbidden on Shabbat. Unlike "work" in the traditional English sense of the word, melachot is usually described as creative activities that exercise control over one's environment, or a skill or craftsmanship. These thirty-nine categories are simply that, categories, and have been expanded, interpreted, and debated over the years.

1. Sowing
2. Plowing
3. Reaping
4. Binding sheaves
5. Threshing
6. Winnowing
7. Selecting
8. Grinding
9. Sifting
10. Kneading
11. Baking
12. Shearing wool
13. Washing wool
14. Beating wool
15. Dyeing wool
16. Spinning
17. Weaving
18. Making two loops
19. Weaving two threads
20. Separating two threads
21. Tying
22. Untying
23. Sewing two stitches
24. Tearing
25. Trapping
26. Slaughtering
27. Flaying
28. Salting meat
29. Curing hide
30. Scraping hide
31. Cutting up hide
32. Writing two letters
33. Erasing two letters
34. Building
35. Tearing down a building
36. Extinguishing a fire
37. Kindling a fire
38. Hitting with a hammer
39. Taking an object from the private domain to the public, or transporting an object in the public domain

DiLLED CARROTS

This is an easy, sweet, delicious side dish. Roz loves them so much she makes them for herself!

SERVES: 6   PREPARATION TIME: 10 MINUTES
COOKING TIME: 25 MINUTES

1 pound carrots peeled and cut in chunks (or 1 pound package peeled mini-carrots)
Salt to taste
1 tablespoon butter
2 tablespoons honey
½ teaspoon dill weed

1. Put the carrots into cold water and bring to a boil.
2. Add a dash of salt, cover, and simmer approximately 20 minutes.
3. When the carrots are tender (not mushy), drain and put them back in the pot.
4. Add the butter, honey, and dill.

✳ This can be made ahead of time and reheated.

✳ Depending on your taste, you can add more honey and dill.

ALLAN'S FAVORITE GARLIC CHICKEN

For most of the time her grandkids spent with her, Grandma Edith lived in a condominium in Coral Gables, Florida. Each floor was open, with the hallways creating a square that traced the outer edge of a large lobby atrium. Suffice it to say, this particular recipe smells so good and so strong that even with fourteen floors of open air, you could still smell it cooking when you stepped off the elevator. To this day, it is one of Roz's husband's favorite dishes of all time.

SERVES: 4–5   PREPARATION TIME: 15 MINUTES
COOKING TIME: AT LEAST AN HOUR

1 whole fryer chicken or 6 breasts with skin and bone
1 stick margarine
Minimum 3–4 cloves garlic, peeled and mashed (the garlic lover can use as many as 6)
Salt and pepper to taste

1. Preheat the oven to 350°F.
2. Wipe the chicken and clean the cavity (see "Cleaning a Chicken," below).
3. Soften the margarine and mix with mashed garlic; add ⅛ teaspoon salt.
4. Put some of the garlic-butter mixture under the skin of the whole chicken or the breast.
5. Spread the leftover garlic butter on the exterior skin, and sprinkle with salt and pepper to taste.
6. Bake 60 minutes or until golden brown, basting often.

Warning: This chicken, while delicious, is for the garlic lover. It is . . . well . . . quite aromatic!

Once and for All: Cleaning a Chicken

Trust us, it's much simpler than it sounds and worth all of the five minutes it takes to do it. Cooking a whole chicken for dinner is amazingly delicious, super-easy, and definitely a proud moment for any beginner cook.

- Place the packaged whole chicken in your clean, empty sink.
- Cut the bag open, remove the chicken, and rinse off all the juices with cold water.
- Reach into the cavity and remove whatever is inside—many times the neck and organ meats will be in a bag, but sometimes the pieces will be loose.
- Once the cavity is empty, rinse the inside once again until the water runs clear.
- Place the chicken on a cutting board (or any other mat) and pat dry.

SWEET-AND-SOUR POPPYSEED DRESSING

This dressing is a little different because of the use of poppyseeds. It's sweet and light and a good alternative to the typical vinaigrette.

MAKES: ABOUT 2 CUPS, SERVES 8   PREPARATION TIME: 5 MINUTES
REFRIGERATE FOR A FEW HOURS

¾ cup sugar
1 teaspoon dry mustard
⅓ cup cider vinegar
1½ tablespoons onion juice
1 cup vegetable oil
1½ tablespoons poppyseeds

Mix all the ingredients together. The dressing will keep in the fridge for 5 to 6 days.

✳ Use a combination of Bibb, romaine, and iceberg lettuce for a delicious salad.

The Burning Question: Everything You Ever Wanted to Know about Kosher Wine

What makes a wine kosher?
Kosher wine is wine that has been created, bottled, opened, handled, and poured only by Jews. There can be no animal products allowed to taint the wine (such as gelatin), all equipment must be specifically used to create kosher wine only, and all must be carefully cleaned.

How do I know if a wine is truly kosher?
The best way to tell is by a symbol on the bottle. The most common kosher wine certifications are "OU" and "OK."

If a non-Jew handles kosher wine, what will happen?
If a non-Jew handles or pours an open bottle of kosher wine, it is no longer considered kosher. A non-Jew can, however, give an unopened bottle of kosher wine as a gift as long as they do not open or drink from the bottle.

I'm having dinner guests from a variety of backgrounds. Are there any loopholes to that rule?
Why, yes there are! If a kosher wine is heated to a near-boiling point, it then becomes *meshuval* or "cooked" and is accepted as kosher no matter who handles it. Meshuval wines are often served at large functions (such as weddings and bar mitzvahs) to allow waiters and caterers to handle kosher wine. Meshuval bottles are usually marked with the abbreviation "Mev."

Kosher Wine Suggestions
Recanati Yasmine Red, Recanati Yasmine White, Yarden Cabernet, Yarden Merlot Yarden Odem Chardonnay

ICE CREAM PiE

This dessert is a true classic in the Marks household and is often requested for birthdays and, well, every holiday we can request it for. It's easier to make than you think and will impress even your most jaded dinner guest. If you really want to go for top honors, pull out your ice-cream maker from the pile of unused wedding gifts and create your own flavors! You will, however, need a 10-ounce round springform pan—basically a pan in which the sides and bottom can be removed. It's easy to find and handy to have in your arsenal.

SERVES: 8   PREPARATION TIME: 3–4 HOURS

GRAHAM CRACKER CRUST

2 cups graham cracker crumbs

2 tablespoons sugar

½ cup melted margarine or butter

1. Preheat the oven to 250°F.
2. In a bowl, mix together all the ingredients.
3. Press the crumb mixture into the bottom and approximately 2 inches up the sides of a springform pan.
4. Bake the crust for 8 minutes.
5. Place in the freezer to cool.

✱ Don't be afraid to make your own crust. It sounds intimidating, but it's truly easy as pie.

CHOCOLATE LAYER

12 1.5-ounce Hershey bars (no nuts) (they usually come in a six-pack)

¼ cup brewed coffee

1. Melt the Hershey bars in the top of a double boiler.
2. After they have melted, add the coffee.

3. Mix well and pour into the bottom of the graham cracker crust.

4. Place in the freezer to chill for about 1 to 1½ hours.

* A double boiler is basically a pot of boiling water with another pot on top. It allows you to heat the contents of the top pot without burning it over direct heat. It's commonly used in melting chocolate.

ICE CREAM LAYER AND TOPPiNG

2 gallons ice cream (your choice of flavors)

Garnish (optional, like whipped cream and fresh raspberries)

1. Soften the first gallon of ice cream and spread three-fourths of the ice cream in the piecrust.
2. Put the pie back in the freezer for about an hour or until frozen.
3. Soften and spread the second flavor (three-fourths of the gallon) onto the first layer.
4. Freeze for another 2 hours.
5. To serve, remove the pie from the springform pan and decorate with whipped cream (or prepared topping) and fresh raspberries.

* Vanilla and chocolate are always "safe" ice cream flavors, but you can combine any two flavors you choose.

* The pie can be made 1 to 2 days ahead of time. Remove from the freezer about 20 minutes before you are planning to serve it, as it is easier to cut when thawed a little.

Simple Shabbat Blessings

Blessing over the Candles

Baruch Atah Adonai, Eloheinu Melech Ha'Olam Asher kid'shanu b'mitzvotav v'zivanu l'hadlik ner shel Shabbat.

Blessed are You, Eternal our God, Sovereign of time and space. You hallow us with Your mitzvot and command us to kindle the lights of Shabbat.

Blessing over the Wine

Baruch Atah Adonai, Eloheinu Melech Ha'Olam, Borei p'ri hagafen.

Praise to You, Eternal our God, Sovereign of the Universe, Creator of the fruit of the vine.

Blessing over the Challah

Baruch Atah Adonai, Eloheinu Melech Ha'Olam, Hamotzi lechem min ha'aretz.

Our praise to You, Eternal our God, Sovereign of the universe, who brings forth bread from the earth.

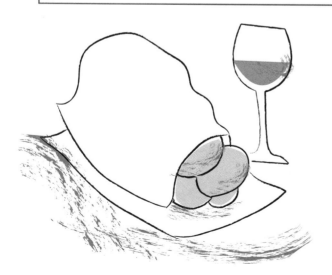

ROSH HASHANAH

"I once wanted to become an atheist but I gave up . . . they have no holidays."

—HENNY YOUNGMAN

Rosh Hashanah is always a major event in the Marks household. For some reason (with the exception of Passover) it always seems to be the holiday where we have the most guests—maybe it's the time of year, or the fact that even the most non-religious Jews somehow come back to the table at the High Holy days. There are always a few extra chairs (and sometimes tables) set out in Roz's living room. To that end, once again we stick to the classics. The egg and caviar spread sets a nice Old World tone for the night. The vegetable soup is a comforting way to warm up an autumn night (and incredibly impressive when made from scratch). Brisket is a staple of any Jewish holiday; this one stays true to the classic ideas of cooking brisket, but was modified over the years by Grandma Edith. Other classics like noodle pudding and roasted vegetables round out the menu (and offer brisket alternatives), with mandelbrot adding a little fun to the dessert course alongside a traditional honey cake.

Note: If you're having a large group, you can easily add any of the chicken dishes and salad dressings from other chapters to satisfy those who shy away from red meat. For smaller groups you may want to cut a dessert and an appetizer.

WINE SUGGESTIONS

Moderately Priced Red:
Guigal Côtes du Rhône (Rhone Valley, France)

Special-Occasion Red:
Yarden Merlot (Israel), Kosher

Moderately Priced White:
Martin Codax Albarino (Rias Baixas, Spain)

Special-Occasion White:
Yarden Odem Chardonnay (Israel), Kosher

THE FACTS

1. Rosh Hashanah literally means "head of the year" or "first of the year" and is often referred to as the Jewish New Year.
2. It marks the beginning of the High Holy Days, the ten-day period of reflection that ends with Yom Kippur.
3. One of the main traditions of Rosh Hashanah is the blowing of the shofar (a hollowed-out ram's horn), which not only calls the worshipers to temple but reminds the congregation to "wake up" from their moral slumber.
4. A main ingredient of a traditional Rosh Hashanah dinner is a round (sometimes raisin-filled) challah, which many say represents the cycle of a new year, as well as apples and honey for a sweet new year.
5. Aside from "Happy New Year," the traditional wish for friends on Rosh Hashanah is to say *"L'shanah tovah tikatevu v'taychataymu"* (may you be written and sealed for a good year), or the shorter *"Shanah tova."*
6. Rosh Hashana usually falls in September or October, depending on the year.

DID YOU KNOW?

- Rosh Hashanah is often thought of as "the birthday of the world," as Jewish tradition says that the world was created on the first day of Tishri.
- Observant Jews often cast off their sins through the custom of Tashlich (literally "casting off"), in which they throw bread or bread crumbs into flowing water.
- This being the twenty-first century, you can now cast off your sins online, with a virtual Tashlich. (Try www.adultjewishlearning.org/ecard.shtml.)
- The holiday "Rosh Hashanah" is never mentioned in the Torah. The holiday is referred to as Yom Ha-Zikkaron (the day of remembrance) or Yom Teruah (the day of the sounding of the shofar).
- The shofar is not blown if the holiday falls on Shabbat.

Make the Everyday Sacred

A message from our favorite rabbi, Rachel Greengrass

There I was—exhausted, covered in sweat and sand, and completely blown away by the beauty that surrounded me. I was in the middle of a spectacular sand desert at an oasis called La Huacachina. My husband and I were honeymooning in Peru and behind the hotel was a huge sand dune, the highest in the area, and I wanted to reach the top. While I had to stop many times I was determined to make it to the top. When we finally did, my breath was literally taken away. I had seen "deserts" before (I lived in Israel for a year) but none like this . . . there was nothing but sand dunes as far as I could see and then there was a beautiful blue watering hole below us. I was overwhelmed, the moment was beyond words. I said a prayer: *"Barukh atah Adonai Eloheinu melekh Ha'Olam, she-hehiyanu v'kiy'manu v'higi'anu la-z'man ha-ze."* (Blessed are You, LORD, our God, Ruler of the universe, who has kept us alive, sustained us, and enabled us to reach this season.)

Even as a rabbi, I was slightly embarrassed when I asked my husband to say this prayer with me, but he says he was glad I did. By saying this prayer that Jews say at happy occasions, the moment was made sacred.

Too often we rely on others to tell us what is deserving of the title "sacred," when in fact, Judaism is intended to be a religion that makes meaning of the lives we are living. Judaism provides avenues for making the everyday sacred, it reminds us not to take the little things for granted, and helps us to transform mundane moments into sacred occasions.

I like to encourage people to think of ways to make Judaism their own. You may not think of yourself as religious or observant, but if you integrate a little Judaism into your everyday lives, it can help you add meaning, make you more grateful, and bring you closer to friends and family. One little thing you might do is to have Shabbat dinner at home. This might simply be a meal with candles, wine, challah, and your favorite dishes and people. It might mean putting your spare change toward those in need (*tzedakah*); or it may be saying a blessing when you see something remarkable or when you do something for the first time. It might mean reminding yourself of your blessings when you wake up in the morning (*Birkot HaShachar*—morning blessings), or reflecting on your day before you go to bed at night (bedtime *Shema*).

The key is to remember that in Judaism there are two kinds of prayer: the *keva*, or fixed prayer—the ones we think of when someone says "prayer" that are in our *siddurim* (prayer books), that we can read and touch; and then there's *kavannah*—prayer with intention or meaning to you personally. Sometimes the prayers we find on the page can be very meaningful, but we should never limit ourselves to the words of others. Prayer should always be a genuine expression, so don't be scared to allow yourself to say "Blessed are you, Adonai our God, who has allowed me to fit back into my skinny jeans," or "Thank you, God, for this fabulous recipe that even my mother-in-law enjoys."

And don't be afraid to go off book on the holidays. Being creative and making new traditions is traditional. My husband and I drink four shots of vodka made from grapes on Passover (same blessing as to the four glasses of wine), and my family does a play of the Exodus instead of reading the story. Shabbat is a day of rest and relaxation, and we are taught to make it an *oneg*—a delight. Think about what that means to you and create some of your own traditions (spa day, anyone?).

The thing to remember is not to be scared, to try new things, and to remember that your Judaism should be a meaningful reflection of your real world experiences and your relationship to God and the world around you. Living a meaningful Jewish life is not an all-or-nothing experience—try to integrate little things here and there, and see how they improve your outlook on life, how they give you comfort, and how they give meaning to the mundane. You don't have to go to an oasis in Peru to find things worth a moment of wonder and blessing; look at your child, or a dear friend, or be appreciative of that warm cozy blanket. Even using this cookbook is a step toward connecting with the Jewish people.

Barukh atah Adonai Eloheinu melekh Ha'Olam. (Blessed are you, Adonai our God, ruler of the universe who has given us the opportunity to find blessings all around us.)

Rabbi Rachel Greengrass was ordained from Hebrew Union College–Jewish Institute of Religion and currently serves as part of the clergy team of Temple Beth Ann in Pinecrest, Florida.

EGG AND CAVIAR SPREAD

An easy inexpensive appetizer that looks impressive because of the caviar. You can serve it individually on lightly toasted French bread rounds (like a Jewish bruschetta!) or in a mound with a basket of toasted french bread rounds, party rye, party pumpernickel, or crackers.

SERVES: 6–8   PREPARATION TIME: 20–30 MINUTES

8 cold hard-boiled eggs
¼ cup finely grated onion
Approximately 1–2 tablespoons mayonnaise
Romaine lettuce, washed and dried (enough to cover your serving platter)
½ cup fat-free sour cream
Small jar of black caviar
Toasted French bread rounds, party rye, pumpernickel, or crackers

1. Mash the eggs and add the grated onion.
2. Add 1½ to 2 tablespoons mayonnaise, enough to make a spread the consistency of egg salad.
3. Chill in the refrigerator for 1 hour.
4. Cover a serving plate with romaine lettuce.
5. Mound the egg mixture into the center of the plate on top of the lettuce, then spread it out to ¼ to ½ inch thick.
6. Put a thin layer of sour cream on top of the egg mixture.
7. Top that with a layer of caviar, then a final dollop of sour cream.
8. Serve with bread and/or crackers.

✳ The best way to hard-boil eggs is to place the raw eggs in a pot and cover them with cold water. Bring to a boil, turn off the heat, and cover the pot. Let sit 14 minutes, then drain. Run the eggs under cold water, let them cool in an ice bath, and peel.

✳ Inexpensive grocery store caviar is perfectly fine for this appetizer.

VEGETABLE SOUP

Far from just a holiday favorite, Roz's vegetable soup is the first thing we all ask for when the weather turns cold (meaning 60s for us Floridians). It's delicious and homey and, though it takes a lot of work, is definitely worth every chop, slice, and simmer. By the way, the meat is used simply to enrich the flavor of the broth and is removed before serving.

SERVES: 8–10   PREPARATION TIME: 1 HOUR
COOKING TIME: 3–4 HOURS

1 tablespoon oil
1 medium onion
1 clove garlic
1–1½ pounds beef short ribs or flanken beef (cut into large pieces)
8 cups water
1 28-ounce can crushed tomatoes
1 28-ounce can diced tomatoes
2 stalks celery, sliced
5 carrots, peeled and cut in chunks
1 zucchini, cut in chunks
1 8–12-ounce package broccoli (frozen or fresh)
1 8–12-ounce package cauliflower (frozen or fresh)
1 8–12-ounce package frozen corn or 1 can corn
1 8–12-ounce package frozen string beans
2 tablespoon kosher salt
1 16-ounce box beef broth (optional)
Salt and pepper to taste

1. Spray a large pot with cooking spray and add the oil. Brown the onion, garlic, and beef until the meat is well browned.
2. Add the water and tomatoes. Bring to a boil and simmer for 1 hour.

3. Add the celery, carrots, zucchini, broccoli, cauliflower, corn, and string beans. Bring to a boil, add salt, and simmer for 3 hours.

4. If the soup is too thick and you prefer a thinner soup, add enough beef broth to get the consistency you like.

5. Traditionally, we remove the beef prior to serving the soup, but you can serve it in the soup or alongside.

✳ This soup freezes well.

REAL WORLD TRADITIONS

"My mom's family is Jamaican so she likes to incorporate some of her culture . . . that explains why we always have rice and peas at Jewish holidays!"

—SUZANNE, NEW YORK CITY, NEW YORK

"My family is weirdly musical, and my grandfather made up a silly song about matzo balls that he would sing when we made them and, of course, ate them. Even though he passed away, the song lives on and we always sing it when we have matzo ball soup at Jewish holidays!"

—ALEESA, COCONUT GROVE, FLORIDA

FRESH STRING BEANS WITH GARLIC BUTTER

Simple, easy, and always delicious, fresh string beans are an easy addition to any menu when you need an extra veggie.

SERVES: 6–8   PREPARATION TIME: 20 MINUTES
COOKING TIME: 10 MINUTES

1–2 pounds fresh string beans
¼ cup margarine, softened
1 or 2 cloves garlic, mashed
Salt to taste

1. Rinse the string beans and cut off both ends.
2. Put the beans in a steamer basket over cold water in a large pot and bring the water to a boil.
3. Cover the pot and turn the heat off. Let the beans steam for 8 to 10 minutes. (They should be crunchy and bright green.)
4. Drain the water and put the beans back in the pot.
5. In a small bowl, mix together the softened margarine and mashed garlic.
6. Stir this mixture into the hot beans. Add salt to taste.

✱ If you don't love garlic, you can also prepare this dish à la our friend Susie: Sauté fresh green beans with just a bit of olive oil and throw in some almond slivers. So delicious!

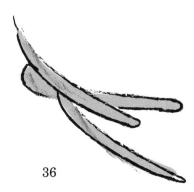

Once and for All: The Sounds of Shofar

The *tekiah* is a single blast.

The *shevarim* is a set of three blasts.

The *teruah* is a set of nine very short blasts.

AUNT JUDY'S SWEET NOODLE PUDDING

A true classic in Jewish cooking, this traditional dish is sure to bring back many memories for young and old alike. This noodle pudding, created by Roz's sister (who happens to be a phenomenal cook), is our favorite.

SERVES: 8   PREPARATION TIME: 30 MINUTES
COOKING TIME: 45 MINUTES

8-ounce package medium-size egg noodles
¾ cup melted margarine
½ cup sugar
1½ cups fat-free sour cream
¾ cup cottage cheese
3 lightly beaten eggs
¾ cup golden raisins (you can also use black raisins)
Pinch of salt

1. Preheat the oven to 350°F.
2. Grease a 2-quart casserole dish, using butter or cooking spray.
3. Boil the noodles, following the directions on the package to cook them al dente.
4. When the noodles are cooked, drain them well.
5. Combine the remaining ingredients in a large bowl and mix thoroughly.
6. Pour the mixture into the greased casserole dish.
7. Bake for 45 to 55 minutes or until golden brown on top.

EDITH'S RED WINE BRISKET

Grandma Edith liked food with a kick. She was creative in the kitchen, always subbing this for that and adding seasoning here and there. For her famous brisket recipe she subbed red wine for water. She also always plugged the brisket with garlic the night before cooking to add some extra flavor. The result was a brisket that we still crave to this day and one that is at the center of almost all our holiday menus.

SERVES: 8–10   PREPARATION TIME: 20–25 MINUTES, OVERNIGHT MARINATING
COOKING TIME: 4 HOURS

1 clove garlic
4–5 pound beef brisket
1 cup kosher red wine (Mogan David or Manischewitz), divided
Salt and pepper
1 tablespoon oil
3–4 carrots, cut into large chunks
1 envelope dehydrated onion soup mix

1. Slice the garlic clove into 6 or 7 thin pieces and "plug" them into the brisket. To do this, make 6 to 7 little cuts into the brisket and stuff the garlic slivers into them.
2. Place the brisket in a dish or plastic storage bag and pour ¼ cup red wine over it. Marinate overnight.
3. The next morning preheat the oven to 325°F. and remove the brisket from the wine. Sprinkle with salt and pepper. Add oil to a skillet and brown all sides of the brisket.
4. Place the brisket in a roasting pan (fatty-side down) and add the carrots. Pour the dry onion soup mix over the brisket along with ¾ cup of red wine. Cover tightly with foil.
5. Bake for 3½ hours, then check the brisket for doneness. If the beef is tender, it's ready; if not, put it back in the oven for another 30 to 45 minutes.
6. Let the brisket cool before slicing. Use the juices in the pan as gravy.

* Buy the first-cut brisket, as it is leaner. It is a little more expensive but well worth it.

* Use Mogan David or Manischewitz wine as these are sweeter than other red wines.

The Burning Questions: Everything You Ever Wanted to Know About Brisket
(Courtesy of Byron Goldenhersh, president, Saveway Food Company, St. Louis)

First, the quality should be choice grade or better, not necessarily prime (too fat), but for extra-high quality one can ask for CAB beef, which most high-end stores like Whole Foods carry. It's an industry acronym and stands for "Certified Angus Beef," which is considered one of the highest-quality breeds of cattle.

Next, decide whether to purchase a whole brisket or just the flat cut. The whole brisket has the fattier "point" portion with a lot of deckle fat, which needs to be removed, along with the outside fat, which needs to be trimmed to ⅛ inch or less, along with the leaner flat portion. Whole briskets weigh about 9 to 12 pounds untrimmed. However, the "point cut portion" is extremely heavily marbled (fat grain), going through the entire point portion of the brisket. When customers at the deli say "that corned beef is too fatty," chances are it's from the point cut. (FYI: The point is primarily used in pastrami, which is traditionally fattier than corned beef, because most customers want their corned beef lean, which comes from the "flat" portion of the brisket. In Jewish delis or kosher-style delis, only brisket is used in making corned beef or pastrami.)

The brisket flat cut is primarily what the shopper sees in the supermarket. It will weigh approximately 4 to 6 pounds and will be lean; only a little trimming of excess fat on the cap and sides will be needed. Once the brisket has been slow-roasted to perfection, it will only be tender if it is sliced correctly. Brisket must be sliced thinly and against the grain. If brisket is not sliced against the grain, it will be tough rather than tender.

HONEY CAKE

It's not Rosh Hashanah without a honey cake. This traditional dessert is a staple of the holiday and would be sorely missed from any menu.

SERVES: 10–12   PREPARATION TIME: 15 MINUTES
COOKING TIME: APPROXIMATELY 1 HOUR

3½ cups presifted all-purpose flour
1 tablespoons baking powder
1 teaspoon baking soda
½ teaspoon salt
3 teaspoons ground cinnamon
½ teaspoon allspice
1 cup vegetable oil
1 cup honey
1½ cups sugar
½ cup brown sugar
3 eggs
1 teaspoon vanilla extract
1 cup brewed coffee at room temperature (can be made from instant coffee)
¾ cup orange juice
½ cup sliced almonds (optional)

1. Preheat the oven to 350°F.
2. In a large bowl whisk together the flour, baking powder, baking soda, salt, cinnamon, and allspice.
3. Make a well in the center of the dry ingredients and add the oil, honey, sugars, eggs, vanilla, coffee, and orange juice.

4. Use an electric mixer on slow speed to mix everything together.

5. Using cooking spray, grease a 10-inch Bundt pan, a 9 x 13-inch baking dish, or three 9- or 10-inch loaf pans (whichever shape pan you prefer).

6. Spoon the batter into the pan and sprinkle the top with almonds (optional).

7. Bake 50 to 60 minutes or until the cake turns golden brown and springs back when gently pressed.

8. Let the cake sit for 20 minutes, then loosen the sides and invert it onto a wire rack to cool completely.

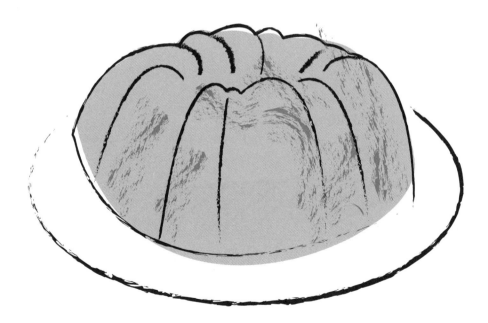

CHOCOLATE CHIP MANDELBROT (MANDEL BREAD)

Rosh Hashanah is a serious holiday, but it's also a time to share with friends and family. To make the holiday more casual, we always bring out large pots of coffee (regular and decaf) and tea as well as milk for the kids and serve up big platters of Chocolate Chip Mandelbrot. Fresh from the oven (or freezer), these delicious cookies are always a hit and are never too heavy after a big dinner. They are also a great gift to bring to someone's home, and a fantastic snack when you want something sweet.

MAKES: 4 DOZEN PIECES (OR MORE)   PREPARATION TIME: 20 MINUTES
COOKING TIME: ABOUT 1 HOUR

4 eggs
1 cup sugar
1 cup oil
½ teaspoon vanilla extract
½ teaspoon almond extract
4 cups flour mixed with 2 teaspoons baking powder
12-ounce package chocolate chips
1½ cups finely chopped walnuts (optional)
2 cups cinnamon sugar (2 cups sugar mixed with 1 tablespoon cinnamon)

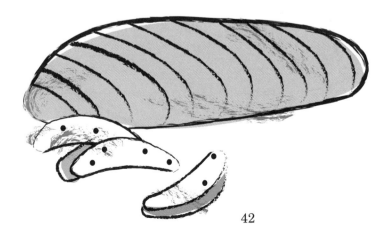

42

1. Preheat the oven to 375°F.
2. Place the eggs into a large mixing bowl, and beat with a fork, whisk, or eggbeater.
3. Add the sugar and continue beating.
4. Beat in the oil and the vanilla and almond extracts.
5. Gradually add (while still beating) the flour and baking powder until mixed together well. It will be thick and sticky. Stir in the chocolate chips and walnuts (optional).
6. Using your hands with a little oil on them, form two or three long and narrow loaves of dough (they should resemble French bread) on a greased baking sheet.
7. Sprinkle the loaves heavily with cinnamon sugar.
8. Bake at 375° for 30 to 35 minutes or until browned.
9. Remove the loaves from the oven and slice on the baking sheet while still warm.
10. Reduce the oven temperature to 275°. Return to the oven, and bake at 275° for another 25 minutes.
11. Cool the mandelbrot on a wire rack.

✳ These cookies freeze really well. I always keep a couple dozen in the freezer.

✳ You can add anything you want to the mandelbrot, so get creative: Raisins, mini-chocolate chips, M&Ms, white chocolate, pecans, or almonds . . . go for it!

Rosh Hashanah Blessings

Barukh atah Adonai, Eloheinu, melekh Ha'Olam asher kidishanu b'mitz'votav v'tzivanu l'had'lik neir shel [shabbat v'shel] yom tov. (Amein)

Blessed are you, Lord, our God, sovereign of the universe Who has sanctified us with His commandments and commanded us to light the candles of the holiday. (Amen)

Shehehiyanu—First Night

Baruch Atah Adonai Eloheinu Melech Ha'Olam, shehechey-nu v'kiy'manu v'higianu laz'man h-zeh.

Blessed are You, Adonai our God, Sovereign of the Universe, Who has granted us life, Who has sustained us, and Who has enabled us to reach this festive occasion.

Apples and Honey

Baruch atah Adonai, Eloheinu melech Ha'Olam, borei p'ri ha-eitz.

We praise You, Eternal God, Sovereign of the Universe, Creator of the fruit of the tree.

Y'hi ratzon milfanecha, Adonai Eloheinu v'Elohei avoteinu v'imoteinu, shetchadesh aleinu shanah tovah um'tukah.

May it be Your will, Eternal our God, that this be a good and sweet year for us.

Wine

Baruch atah Adonai, Eloheinu melech Ha'Olam, borei p'ri hagafen.

We praise You, Eternal God, Sovereign of the Universe, who creates the fruit of the vine.

Bread

Baruch atah Adonai, Eloheinu melech Ha'Olam, hamotzi lechem min ha-aretz.

We praise You, Eternal God, Sovereign of the Universe, who brings forth bread from the earth.

YOM KiPPUR

"I finished what I was writing, pressed 'send' and thought, 'Koufax didn't pitch on Yom Kippur,'
. . . And I haven't worked on Yom Kippur since."

—JANE LEAVY (AWARD-WINNING SPORTSWRITER)

As all of the main courses are basically interchangeable, we thought we might provide a little variation for Yom Kippur. For the most holy and serious of the Jewish holidays, we chose to infuse the menu with a lighter touch; see the Raspberry Cranberry Jell-O Mold. The crabmeat appetizer is always a hit with guests, and the tenderloin and stuffing are stick-to-the-ribs standbys to help fill stomachs for an easier fast. The *kichala,* however, are the true show stopper. For the advanced baker, this dessert is a true old-school Jewish classic sure to impress any and all guests.

WiNE SUGGESTiONS

Moderately Priced Red:
Marques de Caceres Crianza (Rioja, Spain)

Special-Occasion Red:
Catena Malbec (Mendoza, Spain)

Moderately Priced White:
Dashwood Sauvignon Blanc (New Zealand)

Special-Occasion White:
Whitehaven Sauvignon Blanc (New Zealand)

THE FACTS

1. Yom Kippur is arguably the most important holiday of the Jewish year and begins on the tenth day of Tishri.
2. Yom Kippur means "Day of Atonement" and is observed by doing what the name implies. It is believed to be the last chance to change God's judgment of one's deeds in the previous year and his decisions concerning one's fate in the coming year.
3. Yom Kippur is observed by refraining from work, fasting for twenty-five hours (no food or beverages), and spending the day in synagogue, in prayer.
4. The evening service that begins Yom Kippur is called Kol Nidre.
5. Yom Kippur is the tenth and final day of the "Ten Days of Repentance" that begin on Rosh Hashanah.

DID YOU KNOW?

• Yom Kippur has five prayer services rather than the usual daily three, or Shabbat's four.
• Yom Kippur is meant for atoning for sins between man and god, not between people. In order to repent for sins against other men, you must ask for forgiveness from the person himself.
• It is customary to wear white on Yom Kippur as a symbol of spiritual purity.
• It is also customary to give increased charity on the eve of Yom Kippur.
• On Yom Kippur Jews traditionally light a special *Yahrzeit* candle in honor of relatives who have passed away. The candle burns for twenty-four hours and keeps the memory of the deceased alive.

CRABMEAT APPETIZER

Confession: These appetizers are so simple and so delicious that we Markses sometimes make them on any given night. Though they may not be the most calorically responsible, they are easily justified by the fact that they disappear so quickly, you'll only get to eat one or two!

MAKES: 48 PIECES   PREPARATION TIME: 15 MINUTES
COOKING TIME: 10–15 MINUTES

1 stick margarine
1 jar Old English Cheese Spread
2 tablespoons mayonnaise
¼ teaspoon garlic salt
6 ounces drained and flaked crabmeat, fresh or canned
1 teaspoon parsley flakes
⅛ teaspoon seasoned salt
6 English muffins
Paprika

1. Preheat the oven to 400°F.
2. Soften the margarine and cheese spread in a microwave (2 minutes). If you don't have a microwave, warm it in a pan on the stove at low heat.
3. Mix the margarine and cheese together, then add the mayonnaise, garlic salt, crabmeat, parsley flakes, and seasoned salt. Mix well.
4. Separate the English muffins and spread the mixture on the muffins.
5. Place the muffins on a baking pan and put them in the freezer for 15 to 20 minutes to make them easier to cut. Cut each muffin into quarters, put them in a freezer bag, and freeze until ready to use.
6. To serve, place the prepared appetizers on a baking pan; sprinkle lightly with paprika.
7. Bake for 10 to 15 minutes. Serve hot.

✳ You might want to double the recipe and keep extras in the freezer, as they go fast!

CHiCKEN NOODLE SOUP

While our recipe is pretty much the "traditional" chicken soup recipe, a good family friend has a little different take on chicken soup preparation. Leenie's recipe is very similar to the one below, but instead of discarding the celery, carrots, and onion, she removes them and puts them in a food processor, blends them, and puts them back into the soup. Leenie also shreds the chicken and puts that back into the soup as well. It makes for a much thicker and heartier soup.

SERVES: 8–10   PREPARATION TIME: 15–20 MINUTES
COOKING TIME: 3–3½ HOURS

1–2-pound whole chicken (or pieces)
3 stalks celery (ends cut off)
5 peeled carrots
¼ bunch fresh parsley, tied together with string
1 medium onion (you can cut it in half to fit in the pot better)
Approximately 3–3½ quarts water (depends on how big your chicken is)
Salt and pepper to taste
8-ounce package medium-size egg noodles

1. Clean the chicken (see "Cleaning a Chicken," page 23) and place it in an 8-quart soup pot.
2. Add all the other ingredients except the noodles and cover completely with water. Bring to a gentle boil and simmer for 3 to 3½ hours, until the soup turns yellow and the chicken starts to fall apart.
3. When everything is thoroughly cooked, remove the chicken, parsley, onion, and celery. Leave the carrots in the soup.
4. When ready to serve, boil the egg noodles, following the instructions on the package. Drain and add the noodles to the soup.

✳ You can make the soup a day ahead of time and refrigerate it. When cold, the fat will form on top of the soup and you can remove it, thus making a "fat-free" chicken soup.

MOZZARELLA AND TOMATO SALAD

An old steakhouse favorite, this salad is truly as easy as it looks. It's a great alternative to the traditional salad, not only on holidays but any night of the week.

SERVES: 4–6   PREPARATION TIME: 10 MINUTES

3–4 beefsteak tomatoes, or 4–5 vine-ripened tomatoes (whatever is available)
8 ounces fresh mozzarella
1–2 tablespoons extra-virgin olive oil
Salt and pepper to taste
Sprinkle dried basil

1. Slice the tomatoes and mozzarella. (The thickness is a personal preference; just don't make the slices too thin.)
2. Arrange on a serving platter, alternating slices of tomato and mozzarella.
3. Drizzle the salad with olive oil.
4. Season with salt and pepper to taste and sprinkle lightly with basil.

✱ You can make the salad 1 to 2 hours before serving.

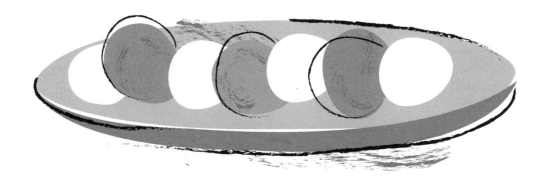

STUFFED FLANK STEAK

This is a great holiday dish, as you can make it earlier in the day or even a day ahead of time and just warm it on low heat in the beef broth. Although a meat dish, it is not a heavy meal, and when fasting the next day, you don't want to stuff yourself the night before.

SERVES: 8–10   PREPARATION TIME: 30 MINUTES
COOKING TIME: 1½ HOURS

1 cup chicken broth
4 tablespoons margarine, divided
3 cups herb-seasoned stuffing bread cubes
3 tablespoons chopped onion
3 tablespoons chopped celery
1 teaspoon salt
¼ teaspoon pepper
2 2-pound flank steaks
¼ cup oil
½–1 cup beef broth
Parsley for garnish

1. For the stuffing, bring the chicken broth to a boil and add 3 tablespoons margarine. When the margarine is melted, add the bread cubes and mix well.
2. In a small pan heat 1 tablespoon margarine and sauté the chopped onions and celery.
3. Combine the sautéed mixture with the bread cubes. Season with salt and pepper.
4. Score the flank steaks diagonally. Heap the stuffing mixture lengthwise down the center of the steaks. Fold in the edges of each steak and tie with string or white thread so it will stay closed.
5. In a large (10- or 12-inch) lidded skillet, brown the stuffed steaks in hot oil.

6. Pour ½ cup beef broth over the browned steaks. Cover and cook over low heat about 1½ hours or until the steaks are tender.
7. To serve, cut the stuffed steaks into slices, place on a platter, and garnish with parsley.
8. Add some extra beef broth to whatever juices are left in the pan and bring it all to a boil. Serve this as gravy on the side.

The Fast and the Famished

It may be tradition, but that doesn't mean fasting for twenty-five hours is easy. We've compiled a few tips to help make an easy fast.

Start early: For a week before the fast, reduce your intake of caffeine, sugar, or other foods that you eat habitually.

Drink up: Drink plenty of water in the days leading up to the fast to prevent dehydration.

Don't push yourself: Jewish law forbids fasting if it puts your health in danger, specifically mentioning the elderly, ill, and those who have just given birth.

Focus on the holiday: Yom Kippur is a solemn holiday and a good time for prayer and reflection.

Don't overeat the night before: A normal-sized meal will keep you feeling full rather than uncomfortable.

RASPBERRY-CRANBERRY JELL-O MOLD

This mold has a long and comic history in our family. For years it was the butt of every holiday joke, then ceremoniously gobbled up the minute it appeared on the table. After a while Roz began to get creative, finding molds in various shapes and patterns to delight her children and nephews . . . and inspire new ways to mock her dish. To this day it never fails to get a laugh. And yes, Eric, Jeff, and David—Andrea in all her kitchen klutz glory dropped the mold on the floor when she was twelve and has never lived it down.

SERVES: 8–10   PREPARATION TIME: 1 HOUR
REFRIGERATE FOR 5 HOURS

2 3½-ounce packages raspberry Jell-O mix
1 cup boiling water
1 cup ice water
1 16-ounce can whole cranberry sauce
1 package frozen raspberries (thawed)
16 ounces sour cream
Romaine, Bibb, or endive lettuce, enough leaves to cover your platter
Fresh raspberries

1. In a medium bowl, dissolve the Jell-O mix in boiling water.
2. After the Jell-O is completely dissolved, add the ice water and mix well.
3. Put the mixture in the refrigerator for about 45 minutes, just until it starts to set (check after 30 minutes).
4. With a hand beater on low, add the cranberry sauce, then the thawed package of raspberries. Beat in the sour cream.
5. Pour the mixture into a mold of your choice, and chill until set. The salad needs at least 5 hours to firm up nicely.

6. To serve, cover a platter with romaine, Bibb, or endive lettuce. Set the salad in the mold upside-down centered on the lettuce-covered platter and remove the mold.

7. Garnish with fresh raspberries.

* Molds are easy to find and come in a variety of fun holiday-themed shapes, so feel free to be creative.

* We spray the mold with cooking spray so the Jell-O mixture slides out nicely.

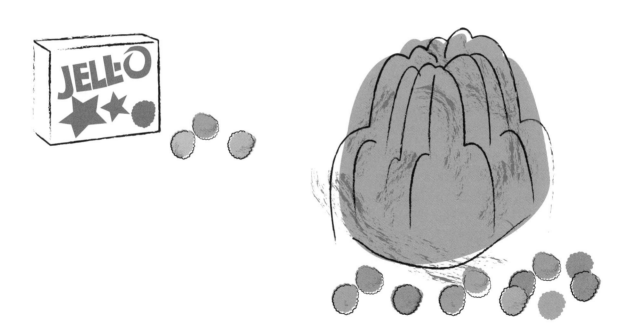

GRANDMA LEAH'S KiCHALA

Leah was Roz's grandmother and Edith's mother, and the originator of many of the baking recipes we still use. She would spend hours making *kichala* but never used a recipe. In fact, when Roz and Edith requested that she hand it over, she had nothing to even give them. Eventually she did her best to verbally pass the basics on to Edith, who then fine-tuned it to the recipe you see below.

MAKES: 6–7 DOZEN   PREPARATION TIME: 4–5 HOURS
COOKING TIME: 50 MINUTES PER BATCH

DOUGH

8 cups flour, plus 1 cup
3 packages Fleischmann's dry yeast
⅓ cup sugar
3 sticks (1½ cups) sweet unsalted butter (cut into chunks for easier melting)
¾ cup sugar
2 cups buttermilk
3 eggs, lightly beaten
1 teaspoon oil

1. Put into an 8-quart pot in this order the flour, the yeast, and ⅓ cup sugar. Do not mix together yet.
2. In a 2-quart pot place the butter, ¾ cup sugar, and buttermilk. Heat on low until the butter is melted and the liquid is hot to the touch, then pour the melted butter mixture over the dry flour mixture in the other pot. Stir with a wooden spoon.
3. Add the beaten eggs and stir until you can form a ball, adding flour from the ninth cup of flour set aside for this purpose.
4. Use your hands to knead and fold over the dough in the pot. When the dough separates from the sides of the pot, it is ready.
5. Rub the teaspoon of oil in the palm of your hands and then wipe lightly all over the ball of dough, which is still in the pot.

6. Cover the pot with a dish towel and leave the dough in a warm place to rise, about 40 minutes.
7. After 40 minutes, punch down the dough and fold it over a few times to reform a ball. Cover again for 30 minutes The dough is now ready to bake.

FILLING
2 cups cinnamon sugar (2 cups sugar mixed with 1 tablespoon cinnamon) for sprinkling
1 10-ounce jar of raspberry preserves
1 cup cinnamon sugar (1 cup sugar mixed with 1½ teaspoons cinnamon) in a cake pan or plate, for dipping

1. Preheat the oven to 200°F.
2. Sprinkle a clean, flat surface with flour.
3. Pinch off a chunk of dough, leaving the remaining dough covered as you roll out each chunk.
4. Place the first chunk of dough on the floured surface and roll into an 8- to 9-inch circle.
5. Sprinkle the circle of dough with cinnamon sugar.
6. Cut the circle into half, quarters, and finally eighths, forming 8 narrow triangles.
7. Put ¼ teaspoon raspberry preserves on the large edge of each triangle. Then roll the triangle tightly into a crescent, or kichala. If some of the preserve seeps out, that's okay.
8. Dip the kichala in cinnamon sugar mixture and place it on a cookie sheet.
9. Repeat with the remaining triangles.
10. Set the pan full of rolled kichala in the 200° oven for 30 minutes to rise.
11. After 30 minutes, raise the temperature to 325°F and bake the kichala for 20 to 25 minutes or until lightly brown. Remove them from the cookie sheet and cool on a wire rack.
12. Repeat this process for each pan, making sure to lower the oven temperature to 200° for 30 minutes to allow the kichala to rise before baking them.

✳ Just open the oven door for a few minutes to cool the oven to 200°.

55

ASPARAGUS WITH LEMON SAUCE

This is a delicious way to serve asparagus. You can put extra lemon sauce in a serving dish on the side. The sauce goes really well with the stuffed flank steak.

SERVES: 4–6   PREPARATION TIME: 5 MINUTES
COOKING TIME: 2–3 MINUTES

2 pounds asparagus
½ teaspoon salt
1 tablespoon margarine
1 cup fat-free sour cream
⅓ cup mayonnaise
1 tablespoon lemon juice
¼ teaspoon white pepper (or black pepper if you don't have white)
Lemon for garnish

1. Put a small amount of water (enough to just cover the asparagus) in a saucepan, add salt, and bring to a boil.
2. Rinse and pat dry the asparagus stalks. Bend each spear to snap off the woody stem; you still might have to cut them to fit into the pot.
3. Boil gently for 2½ to 3 minutes, until the asparagus is bright green and still firm.
4. Drain the asparagus and leave it in the pan until ready to serve.
5. For the sauce, combine the margarine, sour cream, mayonnaise, lemon juice, and pepper, and stir over low heat just until hot. Do not boil.
6. When ready to serve, place the cooked asparagus on a platter and pour the sauce over it.
7. Garnish the plate with thin slices of lemon.

BREAK THE FAST

"Anytime a person goes into a delicatessen and orders a pastrami on white bread, somewhere a Jew dies."

—MILTON BERLE

We Markses are terrible at fasting. In fact, we usually spend the last hour or two of the day deciding what we will eat to break the fast. Traditionally, we break it with the usual fare: bagels, lox, and cream cheese with platters of lettuce, tomato, and onion; kugel; and always tuna salad for my sister-in-law Sarah. If you're hosting a large group, this is the easiest way to go, but you can always substitute deli meats (turkey, pastrami, corned beef, roast beef) if you don't want to go the dairy route. An assortment of bagels is usually easy to secure (stick to plain, whole wheat, and "everything" if you're unsure, and add a rye bread or rolls for the picky), and any good deli can give you the right amount of toppings if you let them know how many people you're expecting. As for the homemade part, we've given you a primer on some easy dishes to add to the table: the tuna with dill, cucumber salad, and fruit for the classicists, and some breakfast favorites like challah French toast and blintzes for those who want something hot. Feel free to borrow from any of the other chapters (the onion kugel is a great addition) to fill out the menu, and don't forget the homemade rugelach. These pastries will bring back memories for just about everyone and are a sweet ending to a long day of fasting. Fresh fruit (See Basics chapter) is always enjoyed and appreciated as well.

WINE SUGGESTIONS

Moderately Priced Red:
Louis Jadot Beaujolais Villages
(Beaujolais, France)

Special-Occasion Red:
Tablas Creek Côte de Tablas Red
(Paso Robles, California)

Moderately Priced White:
Dr L Riesling (Mosel, Germany)

Special-Occasion White:
Sokol Blosser Evolution White (Oregon)

BLINTZ SOUFFLÉ

This is pretty much a classic. We can't think of a breakfast that we've given or been to that doesn't have it. Many serve it with different toppings on the side, such as strawberry or pineapple jam, powdered sugar, sour cream, or fresh raspberries.

SERVES: 8–10 PREPARATION TIME: 10 MINUTES
COOKING TIME: 30–40 MINUTES

½ stick margarine
1 dozen frozen cheese blintzes
4 eggs
¼ cup sugar
1½ cups sour cream
1 teaspoon vanilla
Powdered sugar for garnish or whatever
   you like (jam, sour cream)

1. Preheat the oven to 350°F.
2. Melt the margarine and pour it into the bottom of a 9 x 12-inch glass baking dish.
3. Place the frozen cheese blintzes in the dish, seam-side down.
4. Beat the eggs in a separate bowl and add the sugar, sour cream, and vanilla, mixing well.
5. Pour the mixture over the blintzes.
6. Bake at 350° for 30 to 40 minutes. The top should be lightly browned.
7. Remove the blintzes from the oven, cool a few minutes, and sprinkle with powdered sugar.

5-CUP FRUIT SALAD (AMBROSIA)

This yogurt-dressed fruit salad is an easy and delicious side dish. It goes well with deli sandwiches or bagels and lox. Roz makes it all the time and keeps it in the refrigerator for dessert. This recipe can easily be doubled or tripled for large crowds.

SERVES: 4   PREPARATION TIME: 10 MINUTES
REFRIGERATE FOR 6 HOURS

1 8-ounce container fat-free plain yogurt
1 cup pineapple chunks (drained)
1 cup mandarin oranges (drained)
1 cup marshmallows (miniatures)
1 cup shredded coconut

Mix everything together and refrigerate for at least 6 hours, the longer the better.

TUNA SALAD WiTH DiLL

Long ago we were obsessed with the tuna salad at a restaurant near our old house. We couldn't figure out what made it so delicious. When we finally asked the owner, it turned out that the secret was in the dill. We've been making it this way ever since!

SERVES: 4–6   PREPARATION TIME: 5-10 MINUTES
REFRIGERATE FOR 2 HOURS

2 cans albacore (white meat) tuna
2½ tablespoons mayonnaise (or to taste)
1 tablespoon dill
1 stalk celery, cut into small pieces (optional)

1. Mix all the ingredients and refrigerate for about 2 hours.
2. Serve on a platter covered with romaine lettuce and garnish with seedless red grapes. Or if you prefer, garnish the salad with black and green olives.

✱ This salad can be made a day ahead of time.

60

SARAH'S CHALLAH FRENCH TOAST CASSEROLE

This contribution to our breakfast is usually the first dish to disappear. Special thanks to our daughter-in-law/sister-in-law Sarah for her fantastic recipe!

SERVES: 8–10   PREPARATION TIME: 15 MINUTES (MUST REFRIGERATE OVERNIGHT)
COOKING TIME: 40–50 MINUTES

1 loaf challah, sliced (regular or thick, depending on preference)
7 eggs, beaten
2½ cups low-fat milk
3 tablespoons sugar
1 teaspoon vanilla
½ teaspoon cinnamon
½ cup flour
6 tablespoons brown sugar
¼ teaspoon cinnamon
¼ cup softened butter or margarine

1. Grease a 9 x 13-inch glass baking dish with butter or baking spray, then fill with the slices of challah spread in two layers. Fill in all the spaces with torn pieces of bread if necessary.
2. Mix together the eggs, milk, sugar, vanilla, and cinnamon and pour over the challah.
3. Refrigerate overnight.
4. The next day, bring the dish to room temperature. Preheat the oven to 375°F. Meanwhile, combine the ingredients for the topping (flour, brown sugar, cinnamon, and softened butter) using a fork to make a crumbly mixture.
5. Sprinkle the topping over the casserole.
6. Bake for 40 to 50 minutes until the eggs are set. Serve warm.

* Sprinkle with confectioners' sugar or serve the casserole with maple syrup on the side.

Once and for All: The Question of Kosher

Kosher is one of those terms that are confusing for Jews and non-Jews alike. What's kosher? What's not? Can you be "sort of" kosher? We investigated and have pulled together some of the most basic facts about kosher living.

- Kosher is not a type of cooking.
- Kosher food can be anything—Italian, Chinese, Greek—as long as it's prepared in accordance with Jewish dietary law.
- Kosher food doesn't require a rabbi.
- Many observant Jews say blessings over food prior to eating it, but it is not to make the food kosher. Food is deemed "kosher" as a result of meeting standards set in the Torah that include the separation of meat and dairy, specific rules on slaughtering animals, and instructions on what parts and types of animals can be eaten.

There is a simple explanation for keeping kosher.
- While many people assume the laws of Kashrut are all about health, the truth is that many have no basis in or connection to health concerns. Sure, eating meat and dairy together could interfere with digestion, and laws around kosher slaughter are incredibly sanitary, but the truth is that most people keep kosher because the Torah says so, and for extremely observant Jews that alone is enough.

The main rules are relatively easy to understand.
- The short version: Meat must be from an animal that has cloven hooves and chews its cud (such as cow or goat); fish must have both fins and scales (no to shellfish, yes to tuna, salmon, and herring); birds are categorized into allowable and forbidden (no to hawks, yes to chicken); only animals slaughtered in accordance

with kosher law—meaning no animals that died of natural causes, were killed by other animals, or were slaughtered in a non-kosher fashion—are allowed. Additionally, the blood must be removed, as it is believed to contain the "life" (or soul) of the bird or mammal (fish are exempt).

You must always separate meat and dairy.
• This one is just that simple. In fact, the rules are so strict that even utensils, pots and pans, plates, and dishwashers must be kept apart. Most kosher households will have two sets of everything, including dish towels. All food is categorized into fleishik (meat), milchik (dairy), and pareve (neutral).

The term "keeping kosher" can vary from household to household.
• Standards vary, and while some interpret the laws in the strictest sense, others will make exceptions when they are outside of their home.

There is much more to keeping kosher than what we can cover here, and we encourage you to explore the many kosher Web sites and books that are available to get more detailed information.

HOMEMADE POTATO SALAD

Roz got this recipe from her Mom, Edith, but tweaked it for her own family. Edith added a little more sweet pickle, so that is always an option if you like sweeter potato salad.

SERVES: 8–10   PREPARATION TIME: 45–60 MINUTES
REFRIGERATE FOR 4 HOURS

6 Idaho Russet potatoes
1 cup mayonnaise (I prefer Hellmann's.)
1 cup Miracle Whip
2 tablespoons garlic salt
6 manzanilla olives (green olives stuffed with pimento), cut in small pieces
1 small sweet pickle or sweet gherkin, cut in small pieces
2 cold hard-boiled eggs, peeled
Salt and pepper to taste

1. Peel the potatoes and cut them in chunks.
2. Place the potatoes in a pot of cold water and bring to a boil. Cover the pot.
3. Cook the potatoes for about 15 to 20 minutes in gently boiling water just until they are tender, not mushy.
4. Drain the potatoes well and put them in a bowl to cool in the refrigerator for about 30 to 40 minutes.
5. In the meantime, mix in a bowl the mayonnaise, Miracle Whip, garlic salt, olives, and pickle.
6. Take the potatoes from refrigerator and run a knife through them in the bowl to cut them into smaller pieces.
7. Cut the hard-boiled eggs into small pieces and add them to the potatoes.
8. Pour the mayonnaise mixture over the bowl of potatoes and eggs and mix well. Add salt and pepper to taste.
9. Refrigerate for about 4 hours.

COLESLAW

Making your own coleslaw is easy, economical, and tastes so much better than store-bought. If you like it creamier, just add a little more Miracle Whip.

SERVES: 8–10   PREPARATION TIME: 10 MINUTES
REFRIGERATE FOR AT LEAST 4 HOURS

1–1⅛ cups Miracle Whip
2 teaspoons white vinegar (or apple cider vinegar)
½ teaspoon salt (or to taste)
¼ teaspoon pepper (or to taste)
1 16-ounce package store-bought coleslaw mix (in the produce section)

Mix the Miracle Whip, vinegar, salt, and pepper and pour over the coleslaw mixture. Toss well and refrigerate for at least 4 hours.

65

RUGELACH

Andrea can vividly remember helping her grandmother make these when she was a little girl—cutting the dough into triangles, placing the filling, and then rolling them up and putting them on the baking sheets. Rugelach are made with a light, melt-in-your-mouth dough of cream cheese and sugar, while the kichala dough contains yeast and is heavier and more bread-like. This is a great recipe to involve any children old enough to help, and participation always makes the end result that much sweeter!

MAKES: 6 DOZEN   PREPARATION TIME: APPROXIMATELY 2 HOURS
COOKING TIME: 25–30 MINUTES

DOUGH

8 ounces cold unsalted butter
8 ounces cream cheese
¼ teaspoon salt
¼ cup sugar
1 teaspoon vanilla
2 cups presifted all-purpose flour

1. In a mixing bowl, cream together the butter and cream cheese. Add the salt, sugar, and vanilla and mix until smooth.
2. Add the flour a little at a time and mix until crumbly.
3. Divide the dough into 4 balls, wrap them individually in waxed paper, and refrigerate for 1 to 2 hours.

FiLLiNG

½ cup sugar

1 tablespoon ground cinnamon

1 cup finely chopped walnuts

1 cup cinnamon sugar (1 cup sugar to 1 tablespoon cinnamon), for additional sprinkling

2 cups raspberry preserves

1. Preheat the oven to 350°F.
2. Prepare a baking sheet, greased with cooking spray.
3. Mix together the sugar, cinnamon, and walnuts and set aside. In a separate bowl, prepare the cinnamon sugar for sprinkling.
4. Spread a little flour on a flat surface to keep the dough from sticking. Flour a rolling pin and roll out one ball of dough into a circle until it is about ⅛ inch thick.
5. Using a teaspoon, spread the raspberry preserves all over the dough. Then sprinkle with the cinnamon-sugar-walnut mixture.
6. Cut the dough circle in half, then into quarters. Cut each quarter into three pieces, ending up with 12 pie-shaped wedges.
7. Roll the wedges from the wide end to the narrow end.
8. Place each pastry seam-side down on the cookie sheet.
9. After you have filled the cookie sheet, sprinkle all the rugelach with the cinnamon sugar mixture.
10. Repeat with the remaining 3 balls of dough.
11. Place the rugelach in the oven and bake at 350° for 25 to 30 minutes or until golden brown.
12. Cool a few minutes, then remove it to a wire rack to cool further.

✳ Too much filling leads to a messy rugelach. You will be able to judge the amount of preserves to use after you make your first batch.

CUCUMBER SALAD

Years ago they used to have this simple cucumber salad on the tables at Roz's favorite local deli, and it was one of her favorites. She tried and tried to duplicate it and finally came up with the right combination of ingredients.

SERVES: 8–10   PREPARATION TIME: 15 MINUTES
REFRIGERATE FOR AT LEAST 8 HOURS

2 cups water
1 cup distilled white vinegar
1 cup sugar
2 tablespoons dill weed
5 medium cucumbers, peeled and thinly sliced
½ small onion, thinly sliced
½ red pepper, chopped

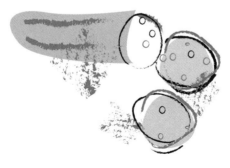

1. Mix the water, vinegar, sugar, and dill in a large container.
2. Place the cucumbers, onion, and red pepper in the liquid mixture.
3. Refrigerate for at least 8 hours.

✳ This salad is best if made at least a day ahead of time. The longer it marinates, the better.

CHANUKAH

"Chanukah is the festival of light, instead of one day of presents we have eight crazy nights!"
—ADAM SANDLER, "THE CHANUKAH SONG"

Probably the most festive and fun of all the modern Jewish holidays, Chanukah is a favorite of every kid (and kid-at-heart) across the globe. From gelt (or chocolate money) to presents, there's no shortage of excitement when it come to celebrating with family—but for many, the true culinary lure of the holiday comes small and fried and topped with applesauce. Yes, the latke. For our Chanukah menu, it is the tried-and-true latke that takes center stage, with an unusual and simple recipe (no flour!) sure to make mouths water. We rounded out the meal with a brisket and a chicken (for those who pass on red meat or have guests who do), some fresh and roasted veggies, and a crisp salad dressing that will leave room for piles of fried potatoes. For larger groups we've thrown in an extra appetizer that you can easily swap in or out depending on tastes and appetites. For dessert we've included a recipe for a fantastic chocolate lace cookie, a treat that goes perfectly with coffee and present opening, and some carrot cake cupcakes sure to fulfill your post-latke sweet tooth.

WINE SUGGESTIONS

Moderately Priced Red:
Fess Parker Frontier Red (Santa Barbara, California)

Moderately Priced White:
Frei Brothers Chardonnay (Sonoma, California)

Special-Occasion Red:
D'arenberg Foot Bolt Shiraz (Australia)

Special-Occasion White:
Newton Red Label Chardonnay (Napa, California)

REAL WORLD TRADITIONS

"Our family has gotten so big via marriages and babies that now we only buy presents for all the kids. When it comes to the adults, we do two things. The first is a small $30 gift that we use in a 'Dirty Santa-esque' exchange: basically, you draw a number and can steal the gift from anyone before you. For the second, we draw names at Thanksgiving dinner and put a higher price tag (usually between $100 and $150), then we reveal the gifts and the giver on the first night of Chanukah. It's a lot of fun and saves us all a lot of stress."

—STACI, MIAMI, FLORIDA

"Chanukah 1986, I was four and my sister was three. My entire family had driven from Seattle to LA to visit our grandparents for Chanukah. One evening, as we were lighting the candles, my mother, sister, grandmother, and I were hovering around saying the prayer back and forth in both Hebrew and English. At the end of reciting the English, my little sister, in her three-year-old squeaky voice, screamed 'CHANUKAH!!!!!!' She yelled it as though she had just won a million dollars. In her three-year-old world, this particular night of Chanukah was the best night of her life. Ever since, as an entire family we always yell 'CHANUKAH!!' with just as much gusto as my sister did in 1986. Now twenty-five and twenty-seven, my sister and I will never say the prayer for lighting the Chanukah candles in a boring fashion, and I honestly hope our silly little tradition will be passed on to our own children (when they come around . . .)."

—MEGAN, CORVALLIS, OREGON

"I grew up in Israel where Chanukah is actually much more simple than here in the U.S. When my son was able to REALLY understand the holiday, we made a safe menorah using crayons instead of candles. At night, we light two menorahs—one for each child. My kids have a great time choosing the candle colors and setting it up. We do the prayers, light the candles, and then sing songs together in Hebrew, English, and Spanish. It's a lot of fun!"

—EFRAT, MIAMI, FLORIDA

"We have a tradition for giving Chanukah gifts by choosing envelopes. When my two children were young, I would fill sixteen envelopes (one for each night for each child) with different amounts of money, all of which would add up to a certain total (usually $50 or $100). Each night they would choose one envelope . . . sometimes they would get $20 and sometimes only $1. It became a game to see who could end up with the bigger total by the last night. Now that they are grown, with families of their own, we fill the envelopes with different gift cards to bookstores or coffee shops or restaurants. It's fun to see who gets what, and the suspense of which envelope to choose never gets old!"

—JOYCE, CLEARWATER, FLORIDA

"Every year we get together to celebrate Chanukah with friends and family, and everyone brings their own menorah. We light all the candles together, sing songs, and say the prayers and then take TONS of pictures."

—MYRA, MIAMI, FLORIDA

THE FACTS

1. Chanukah is observed for eight days beginning on the twenty-fifth day of the month of Kislev (a date that roughly correlates to sometime in December).
2. Chanukah commemorates the miraculous victory of the Maccabees over the pagan Syrian-Greeks who ruled Israel.
3. Chanukah has two meanings: The first is "dedication," for it was on Chanukah that the rededication of the Holy Temple took place. The second meaning derives from Chanu ("they rested"—meaning the Maccabees) and Kah ("on the twenty-fifth").

DID YOU KNOW?

- For more than twenty years an amateur cook in Long Island has organized a Latke Festival.
- The Jones Soda Company created a Chanukah 2007 latke soda.
- One legend says Judah Maccabee and his soldiers ate latkes to fortify themselves on the way to battle the Syrians.
- Yes, you can make latkes with sweet potatoes.
- There is an annual Great Latke–Hamantash Debate among academic scholars.
- The menorah is meant to be displayed for all to see. These days that means either the front window of the home or the room inside that gets the most traffic.

Once and for All: Lighting the Menorah

Chanukah candles should be lit when stars first appear in the sky. They are placed in the menorah starting on the far right side and moving left each night. They are lit, however, from the left to the right. Whew.

It's Not a Party without Cocktails . . .

At least, that's what we always say! When your crowd is in a festive mood, nothing raises the fun factor more than specialty drinks. Most of us aren't in the position to hire a bartender (though it's never a bad idea for a large crowd), but that's not a problem. There are plenty of drinks that are easy to make and delicious to taste that will appeal to a wide range of guests. Below we offer three takes on non-traditional holiday cocktails from two of our favorite restaurants. The Pink Ginger Skyy Martini is a festive, fun, colorful option that's simple and straightforward. For larger groups you can't go wrong with sangria (delicious, fun, and self-serve), so we've provided you with both a red and white option. For the best sangria, prepare it in advance and let it sit in the fridge for at least a couple of hours. The fruit will soak up the liquid and make the drink even better.

PINK GINGER SKYY MARTINI
(Courtesy of Pacific Time executive chef/owner Jonathan Eismann)

MAKES: 1 DRINK

2 ounces Skyy vodka
½ ounce Triple Sec
1 lime wedge
1 splash juice of fresh ginger, poached in port or kosher red wine

Add the vodka, Triple Sec, a squeeze of fresh lime, and a splash of ginger juice to a cocktail tumbler with ice; shake well. Strain into a martini glass.

✳ Sangria is normally made in large batches. Thus, you should double these recipes.

RED SANGRIA
(Courtesy of Brosia restaurant owner Scott Engelman and Chef Arthur Artilles)

SERVES: 3–4

16 ounces Malbec or dry kosher red wine
2 ounces of apricot brandy
2 ounces of peach schnapps
Touch of Triple Sec
1 apple, diced
1 orange, diced

Mix all the ingredients and let sit for couple of hours in the refrigerator to marinate the fruit. Pour into a large rocks glass with lots of ice.

WHITE SANGRIA
(Courtesy of Brosia restaurant owner Scott Engelman and Chef Arthur Artilles)

SERVES: 3–4

16 ounces Pinot Grigio or kosher white wine
2 ounces apricot brandy
2 ounces peach schnapps
Splash of Triple Sec
1 orange, diced
4 strawberries, diced
Splash of Cava or any inexpensive sparkling wine

Mix all ingredients and let sit for couple of hours in the refrigerator to marinate the fruit before serving. Pour into a large rocks glass with a lot of ice. Finish off with splash of Cava.

FRUIT AND CHEESE APPETIZER

When serving a relatively heavy meal, we generally prefer to serve a lighter appetizer. December is apple and pear month. We like Gala apples, and Bartlett pears, but it really is personal preference. Granny Smiths are great but a little tart, and Red Delicious are sweet but not as crunchy. Also, if your grocery store has seedless red grapes, they are fabulous to serve.

Red grapes are sweeter than green and look prettier when serving.

First, slice the fruit into wedges and serve with the following cheeses, which you can buy at any grocery store or wine and cheese shop: sharp Cheddar (get a good one—we like Cabot or Montgomery's—it makes a difference); Monterey Jack; havarti; Colby; Gruyère; and Roquefort (which goes great with apples).

Put the cheeses out on a large serving platter or cheese board before everyone comes, and when guests start arriving place apples and pears at opposite ends of the platter with the cheeses in the middle. Serve a variety of crackers alongside in a basket.

✳ To keep apples and pears from browning for at least 1 or 2 hours, take a mist bottle and fill it with 1 quart ice-cold water and 2 tablespoons lemon or lime juice. After cutting the fruit, mist it lightly and keep it refrigerated until right before serving. There are commercial products you can buy as well to keep fruit from browning for a couple of hours.

✳ Faced with a spread of cheeses, it never hurts to ask for help when choosing a good pairing—we find that most shop owners are more than happy to impart their knowledge.

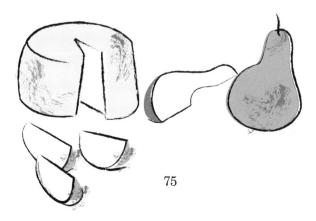

HONEYED CHiCKEN WiNGS

For some groups, fruit and cheese just won't cut it as an appetizer. This recipe is a little messy and a lot delicious, and seriously could not be easier to whip up.

SERVES: 8–10   PREPARATION TIME: 10 MINUTES
COOKING TIME: 1 HOUR

3–4 pounds chicken wings (separated, no tips)
½ cup soy sauce
2 tablespoons vegetable oil
2 tablespoons ketchup
1 clove garlic, chopped
1 cup honey

1. Preheat the oven to 350°F.
2. Grease a 9 x 13-inch baking pan with cooking spray or a little oil, and place the chicken wings in the bottom.
3. Mix together the remaining ingredients and pour over the chicken.
4. Bake uncovered for 1 hour or until the chicken is done (and a golden brown color) and the sauce has caramelized.

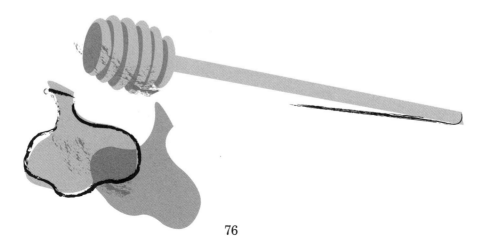

Chanukah Playlist

Chanukah is a social holiday, and the time of year just begs for parties, parties, and more parties. For those sick of the holiday classics, we asked our own musical experts, brothers Nick and Peter Rosenberg, for an updated take on the old Chanukah playlist. So if your taste runs more Snoop Dogg than Rudolph, here are their suggestions to spice up your party.

Eight Songs for Eight Nights

1. "Shamrocks and Shenanigans"—House of Pain: Okay, the title doesn't scream Chanukah, but I have thousands of hip-hop records, and I can assure you that this is the only one that has a menorah reference. "If I were a Jew I would light the menorah," Everlast says. Needless to say, this is a great way to kick off your party. It should ease any of your overbearing relatives' concerns that your choice of tunes isn't Chanukah friendly. And if you must play House of Pain's anthem, "Jump Around," while you're at it, play Pete Rock's remix—it's a classic.

2. "Donuts"—Jay Dee aka J Dilla: There are a million reasons to love Chanukah. When I was a kid the best thing was the presents, but as I got older the presents went from being Transformers and GI Joe to socks and three-packs of boxers. It was at this point that the jelly donuts aka *soufganiot* became my favorite thing about Chanukah. And "Donuts" is one of my favorite things about J Dilla (RIP), my favorite producer of all time. Not only does this album relate to Chanukah with its allusion to the most delicious of Chanukah foods, but the bonus for you is that this album is all instrumentals and, as a result, certain not to offend your Aunt Pearl. Dilla's "Donuts" is not a reference to the greatest food of all time, but rather the 45s that Dilla sampled to make this phenomenal album.

(continued)

3. "Fried Chicken"—Nas, featuring Busta Rhymes: This one probably will offend Aunt Pearl, but it's a must. This is a song about both how delicious and how unhealthy fried food is. Probably not something you want to hear about as you dunk your tenth latke in a tub of sour cream. But then again, if you care, you're probably not going to eat ten latkes anyway and I don't even want you at my Chanukah party.

4. "Songs in the Key of Hanukkah"—Erran Baron Cohen: Yes, he's related to Borat, Ali G, and Bruno's alter ego, Sacha Baron Cohen—he's his brother. And he's a DJ, producer, and composer as well, who put out an album of offbeat hip-hop–influenced Chanukah music, complete with a new up-tempo version of "Chanukah Oh Chanukah," sure to get your preschool-age attendees amped. Featured prominently on the album is Y Love, an African-American rapper who rhymes in Yiddish. Only in America. Or England. Or something.

5. Anything by Asher Roth: Not only does he exuberantly shout "mazel tov" in his version of Jay Z's "Roc Boys," but if any of your guests object to what they are listening to, just tell them the name of this artist is Asher Roth, and that should put any objection to rest. They'll think it's the president of their shul's men's club and probably leave you alone.

6. "I Got Five on It"—The Luniz (pronounced, "loonies"): The name of this group could apply to any gathering of more than five Jewish family members for Chanukah, or any other Jewish holiday for that matter. Plus, when I was young, a kid in my Hebrew school, Drew Shteynfarb, told me that "having five on it" was a reference to participation in high-stakes street dreidel games.

7. "Brooklyn Queens"—3rd Bass: MC Serch of 3rd Bass is not only a Jew, but arguably, the greatest Jewish rapper of all time and an encyclopedia of hip-hop history and lore. Not to mention, the original version of this song was called "Great Neck Princesses," which was rejected by the label because it wasn't street enough. Okay, the second part isn't true. But MC Serch and 3rd Bass are definitely worth checking out for your Chanukah playlist.

8. "Back to the Grill Again"—MC Serch: Did I mention that Serch is Jewish? This is Serch's solo hit, also a classic. The refrain of this track, "back to the grill again, the grill again" during the chorus will remind you to check on those latkes and brisket. Serch definitely knew about the dangers of a house full of hungry Jews.

Peter Rosenberg is a radio personality on Hot 97 in New York City and the host of "Noisemakers" at the 92Y Tribeca, where he regularly interviews the brightest talent in the hip-hop world. Nick Rosenberg is a New York–based entertainment lawyer and avid hip-hop fan.

SWEET AND TANGY BRISKET

A true original out of Roz's kitchen, Sweet and Tangy Brisket was born of her own frustration in re-creating a famous chef's brisket recipe (let's call him Mobby Play). Thinking she saw it on a morning show, Roz searched the Internet far and wide for the recipe before enlisting the help of her husband, Allan, and Andrea in her quest. No dice. Desperate to stop Roz's endless searching, Andrea took it upon herself to e-mail said chef asking for the recipe and including ingredients from Roz's memory. Within days the chef responded. He had never heard of such a recipe. Undaunted, Roz started experimenting, and the result was a sweet and savory treat we enjoy every year.

SERVES: 10–12   PREPARATION TIME: 20 MINUTES
COOKING TIME: 3–3½ HOURS

1 clove garlic
3–4 pounds flat- or first-cut brisket
1 tablespoon oil
Pepper
1 32-ounce bottle of ketchup
1 cup light or dark brown sugar
½ cup green olives
¼ cup capers
½ cup golden raisins
5–6 carrots, peeled and cut in half

1. Preheat the oven to 350°F.
2. Peel the garlic clove and slice it really thin.
3. "Plug" the brisket all over with the garlic slivers on one side (you can do this either the day before or right before cooking).
4. Heat a large skillet with oil, enough to just cover the bottom.
5. Rub the brisket all over with pepper.
6. Brown the brisket on both sides. Each side should take 2 to 3 minutes.

7. While the brisket is browning, mix together the ketchup, brown sugar, olives, capers, and raisins in a large bowl.

8. When the brisket is browned on both sides, place it in a large baking dish. Place the carrots around it and pour the ketchup mixture on top. Cover tightly with aluminum foil.

9. Bake the brisket for 3 to 3½ hours. You should be able to pull it apart with a fork when it's done.

10. Cool and slice the brisket. Serve the sauce on the side.

✳ This dish can be prepared weeks ahead of time and frozen. You can freeze it (unsliced) in the baking dish. Make sure it is covered tightly for the freezer.

What's in a Name?

There are many, many, many ways to spell Chanukah. A few examples:

Chanukkah	Chanukah	Hanukkah
Channukah	Hanukah	Hanuka
Chanuka	Hannukah	Hanukka

So, which one is right? Although Chanukah is the most common spelling in the United States, they are all correct. There is no true, approved spelling when translating from Hebrew to English.

ANDi'S SPRiTE-ROASTED LEMON-PEPPER CHiCKEN

In Florida the grill is king. Unfortunately, from May through August, so is the rain. This recipe originated on the grill as a classic beer-can chicken. One fine day, however, a thunderstorm forced us all inside, and in a moment of desperation Andrea threw the chicken in the oven. Guess what? It was even better. Besides, even though brisket is always delicious, sometimes you need something a little different to mix it up.

SERVES: 4–6   PREPARATION TIME: 25 MINUTES
COOKING TIME: 2–3 HOURS

1 small whole chicken
3 cloves garlic
Olive oil
Seasoned salt (I like McCormick Season All.)
Garlic powder
Lemon pepper
Salt
Pepper
1 can of liquid, any size (beer, Sprite . . .)
½ cup low-sodium chicken broth

1. Preheat the oven to 425°F.
2. Spray a small roasting pan with cooking spray and set it aside.
3. Clean the chicken and pat it dry (see "Cleaning a Chicken," page 23).

* Take the tops off all your spices before starting to season; it will make your life a lot easier when your hands are covered in olive oil.

4. Chop the garlic into small pieces and set it aside.

5. Cover the chicken with olive oil, making sure to get under the skin.

6. Season the chicken with as much or as little seasoning as you want (the more the better), using a good amount of the lemon pepper and making sure to get it under the skin (you can use a pastry or basting brush to make it easier).

7. Place the garlic under the chicken skin.

8. Empty out about one-third of the liquid in the can. Place the can inside the roasting pan and set the chicken on top, using the legs to form a tripod so it is standing up straight.

9. Pour the chicken broth into the bottom of the pan and place the chicken in the oven.

10. Roast the chicken at 425° for 30 minutes. Then turn the oven down to 375° and continue roasting for about 1 hour or until the juices run clear. During the last 30 minutes, use a baster to pull up the liquid in the bottom of the pan and baste the chicken about every 7 to 10 minutes.

11. Remove the pan from the oven, remove the can from the chicken cavity, and carve.

✳ Be very careful removing the can from the chicken. It's incredibly hot and requires a two-person effort: one to hold the chicken and one the can.

FLOURLESS POTATO PANCAKES

These are the best latkes you have ever had. Seriously. One of Roz's original holiday visitors may have expressed it best when convincing her husband to fly to Miami for the holiday. Said Ellen: "They are what happens to McDonald's hash browns when they die and go to heaven."

SERVES: 10–12 (OR MORE)   PREPARATION TIME: 45 MINUTES
COOKING TIME: 45 MINUTES

12–13 medium Idaho Russet potatoes
1 large onion
4 eggs
Vegetable oil
Salt

1. Peel the potatoes. (If prepping them ahead of time, put them in ice water to keep them from turning brown.)
2. Grate the potatoes, then the onion, in a Cuisinart.
3. Mix them together and add the eggs.
4. Pour vegetable oil into a large skillet, enough to fill the pan about one-eighth of the way up the sides. Heat the oil over medium-high heat. Splash a drop of water into the oil; if it sizzles, the oil is ready.
5. Drop the potato mixture (one large tablespoonful per latke) into the hot oil and fry until golden brown and crisp (about 3 to 4 minutes per side). Cook 3 or 4 in a batch, making sure they don't touch each other.
6. Always make sure you have enough oil in the pan. After about two batches you will probably need to add oil.

7. When the latkes are browned and crisp, transfer them from the pan to a brown paper bag to drain excess oil.

8. Sprinkle with salt to taste and serve.

9. If the latkes were made a little ahead of time, place them on a baking sheet and reheat them in a 400–425°F oven until ready to serve.

* The ratio of eggs per potatoes is 2 eggs for every 6 or 7 potatoes. If making latkes for a smaller group, use 5 or 6 potatoes, 2 eggs, and half of a large onion or 1 small onion.

It's a Dangerous Job, but Someone's Got to Do It
The Secrets of Latke-Making

It may not rank up there with Alaskan king crab fishing, but making latkes is a dangerous job. The use of hot oil and the need for a lot of flipping and moving means concentrating on the task at hand is key. Follow these simple tips to keep your kitchen safe:

- Clean oil spills immediately.
- Invest in a splatter guard.
- Keep oven mitts close by.
- Keep pets and small children out of the kitchen
- Know the location of the closest fire extinguisher, or have a pan lid or box of baking soda handy to smother the fire.

The Burning Question: What Should I Put on My Latkes?

Sure, sour cream and applesauce are the traditional toppings for latkes. But what happens when we think outside the box? People can get pretty creative when it comes to topping fried potatoes. A hot trend in Chanukah cooking is the "Latke Bar." Setting up stations allows guests to customize this traditional favorite to suit their own palate. Below we've gathered a few traditional and non-traditional latke toppings, but feel free to add your own.

Applesauce
Sour cream (regular or light, perhaps
  with a dash of vanilla)
Mango chutney
Salsa
Cranberries
Jam
Marmalade
Yogurt
Honey

Caramelized onions
Sautéed shredded carrots
Sautéed or fresh zucchini
Grilled mushrooms
Artichokes
Goat cheese
Ketchup (yes, ketchup)
Caviar
Oven-roasted tomatoes

EASY HOMEMADE PEAR-INFUSED APPLESAUCE

Store-bought applesauce can be great in a hurry, but to truly impress guests, why not take a simple recipe and infuse it with a hint of pear? Trust us, it's easier than you think—
it just sounds gourmet!

SERVES: 4   PREPARATION TIME: 15 MINUTES
COOKING TIME: 45 MINUTES

12 apples (Gala, Fuji, Macintosh)
2–3 ripe pears
Cinnamon sugar (2 cups sugar to 1 tablespoon cinnamon)

1. Preheat the oven to 350°F.
2. Peel, core, and cut the apples and pears into eighths.
3. Spray a medium-size baking dish with a cooking spray.
4. Place the fruit wedges in the dish and cover tightly with aluminum foil.
5. Bake for 45 minutes or until the apples and pears are soft, but not mushy. (You can check by poking them with a fork after 45 minutes.)
6. When the fruit is tender, remove it from the oven. Cool.
7. In the same dish, mash and mix the apples and pears with a fork. Depending on how sweet the fruit is, add cinnamon sugar to taste
8. Chill for a couple of hours and serve.

✳ If you don't want to include a pear flavor, just delete the pears from the recipe for a delicious classic applesauce.

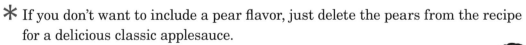

ROASTED VEGETABLES

A low-calorie and easy side dish that goes with any meal. You can put in any combination of your favorite veggies.

SERVES: 6–8   PREPARATION TIME: 30 MINUTES
COOKING TIME: 30 MINUTES

1 medium zucchini, cut in chunks
1 medium summer squash, cut in chunks
1 small onion, cut in chunks
1 medium red bell pepper, cut in chunks
1 small eggplant, cut in chunks
8–10 cherry tomatoes
8-ounce package mushrooms, stems cut off
¼ cup olive oil
½ teaspoon salt
¼ teaspoon pepper
½ teaspoon garlic salt

1. Preheat the oven to 425°F.
2. Mix all the ingredients and place in a large baking or roasting pan.
3. Roast uncovered for 30 minutes.

✱ Never rinse mushrooms. To clean them use a damp paper towel and wipe them off.

CREAMY VINAIGRETTE DRESSING

Dinner isn't dinner in the Marks house without a salad. It lends a light, crisp touch to an otherwise heavy dinner and adds another option for those non-brisket eaters among us (I know, we don't understand them either . . .). Mixing iceberg lettuce with romaine and chopping red peppers, cucumbers, and fresh tomatoes sets off the homemade lemony dressing we added below.

MAKES: ABOUT ¾ CUP, SERVES 6   PREPARATION TIME: 10 MINUTES

1 teaspoon salt
1 teaspoon pepper
½ teaspoon sugar
1 teaspoon Dijon mustard
1 teaspoon lemon juice
2 tablespoons tarragon vinegar
8 tablespoons vegetable oil
2 tablespoons olive oil
1 egg
5–6 mashed anchovies (optional)

1. Mix the first 8 ingredients together.
2. Beat the egg and add the above mixture to it. Beat well.
3. If you like, you can add mashed anchovies to the dressing.

✳ The dressing is really delicious on romaine lettuce and radicchio. Leftover dressing can be stored in the fridge for up to a week.

CARROT CAKE CUPCAKES

This family recipe has been wowing visitors for decades. Traditionally served as a cake, we translated the recipe into cupcake form to make it a little more fun for the holidays, but it's just as delicious either way.

SERVES: 10–12   PREPARATION TIME: 30–45 MINUTES
COOKING TIME: 45–55 MINUTES

2 cups sugar

1 cup oil

4 eggs

2 cups flour

3 cups peeled and grated carrots (do not use peeled mini-carrots)

2 teaspoons baking soda

2 teaspoons cinnamon

1 teaspoon salt

1. Preheat the oven to 325°F.
2. Line a standard muffin pan with 2-inch cupcake liners.
3. Mix and beat together the sugar and oil.
4. Beat in the eggs.
5. Combine the flour, baking soda, cinnamon, and salt.
6. Stir the flour mixture into the creamed mixture.
7. Add grated carrots.
8. Pour the batter into cupcake liners until a third full.
9. Bake for 25–30 minutes or until golden brown
10. Cool and then frost with cream cheese frosting.

* For a traditional carrot cake, pour the batter into two greased 8-inch round cake pans and bake at 325°F for 45 to 55 minutes, or until the cakes are golden brown and spring back when touched.

CREAM CHEESE FROSTiNG

Cut this in half for cupcakes, but use the full amount if making a cake.

8-ounce package of Philadelphia Cream Cheese
1 stick margarine or butter
1 teaspoon vanilla
1 16-ounce box confectioners' sugar
1 cup chopped nuts (optional)

1. Cream together the cream cheese, butter, and vanilla.
2. Gradually beat in the powdered sugar till smooth. Frost the cake and sprinkle with the nuts, if you like.

✳ When icing a cake, before removing the first cake layer from the pan and placing it on a cake plate, put strips of waxed paper around the edges of the cake plate and place the cake on top of the paper. When you are icing the cake, the excess icing will end up on the waxed paper so that when you pull the paper away, your cake plate will be clean.

✳ When cool, remove one cake from cake pan and ice it, then remove the second cake, place it on top of the first, and ice the top and sides of the cake.

✳ If you make the carrot cake a day ahead of time, keep it in the refrigerator. The cake also freezes well. After cooling it completely in the refrigerator so the icing hardens, wrap the cake in waxed paper and then in aluminum foil and place in the freezer. The waxed paper will keep the icing from sticking to the foil.

CHOCOLATE CHiP LACE COOKiES

Cookies, chocolate, and oats . . . what could be better?
These cookies are lighter than traditional chocolate chip cookies and great to bring out when
extra guests stop by during the holidays.

MAKES: APPROXIMATELY 3 DOZEN   PREPARATION TIME: 20 MINUTES
COOKING TIME: 10 MINUTES

⅔ cup flour
½ teaspoon salt
½ cup rolled oats (old-fashioned oatmeal)
1½ sticks sweet unsalted butter, softened
⅔ cup light brown sugar
⅔ cup white sugar
1 large egg, lightly beaten
2 cups chopped pecans or walnuts
⅔ cup chocolate chips

1. Preheat the oven to 350°F. Line a baking sheet with parchment paper.
2. Combine in a bowl the flour, salt, and oats.
3. In mixing bowl cream the butter with the sugars, then add the egg.
4. Stir the flour mixture into the creamed mixture and add the nuts and chocolate chips.
5. Drop the dough by teaspoonsful onto the parchment paper-covered baking sheet.
6. Bake the cookies for 8 to 10 minutes.

* These cookies make a great gift during the holidays.

The Game: Dreidel

The dreidel is a four-sided top and one of the most recognizable symbols of Chanukah. Many believe it dates back to Greek-Syrian times, when Jews were forbidden to study Torah. Legend has it that children would keep the tops on them to pull out and play with should enemy patrols come by.

The Players: Anyone!

The Pieces: A dreidel and a variety of candy (such as M&Ms).

The Rules: Each player starts off with a different color M&M (or other nut or candy). Each player puts one of his or her pieces in the pot. Each player spins the dreidel and does whatever the letter dictates:

> "Nun," he collects nothing.
>
> "Gimel," he wins the entire pot.
>
> "Hey," he gets half the pot.
>
> "Shin," he has to put one of his own pieces in the pot.

Continue until someone wins the entire contents of the pot.

SING!

"I Have a Little Dreidel"

I have a little dreidel,
I made it out of clay.
And when it's dry and ready,
Oh dreidel I shall play.

(Chorus)
Oh dreidel, dreidel, dreidel,
I made it out of clay;
And when it's dry and ready,
Then dreidel I shall play.

It has a lovely body,
With legs so short and thin.
And when it gets all tired,
It drops and then I win!

(Chorus)

Chanukah Songs

"Ma'oz Tzur (Rock of Ages)"
Rock of Ages, let our song praise your saving power.
You amid the raging throng were our sheltering tower.
Furious they assailed us, but your help availed us.
And your word broke their sword when our own strength failed us.

"Oh Chanukah"
Oh Chanukah oh Chanukah, A Festival of Light
A holiday, a jolly day, for every girl and boy
Spin the whirling Dreidel, all night long
Eat the sizzling Latkes, sing a happy song

(Chorus)
And while we are singing, the candles are burning low
One for each night, they shed a sweet light, to remind us of days long ago.
One for each night, they shed a sweet light, to remind us of days long ago.

Oh Chanukah oh Chanukah, come light the menorah
Let's have a party, we'll all dance the horah
Gather 'round the table, we'll give you a treat
Dreidels to play with and latkes to eat

(Chorus)

"Not By Might, Not By Power"
Not by might and not by power,
but by spirit alone shall we all live in peace.
but by spirit alone shall we all live in peace.
The children sing, the children dream,
and their tears may fall, but we'll
  hear them call
and another song will rise,
another song will rise,
another song will rise!

PASSOVER

"Let me tell you the one thing I have against Moses. He took us forty years into the desert in order to bring us to the one place in the Middle East that has no oil!"

—GOLDA MEIR

Passover is all about the seder, meaning traditional fare such as *charoset,* gefilte fish, and matzo ball soup. For "the Festive Meal" (as we Markses like to call it), we went with a delicious roast turkey (though you can sub in any of the brisket or chicken recipes) alongside fresh vegetables, and Passover matzo rolls. For dessert, Aunt Frieda's nut cake is always a winner, but Passover brownies and almond macaroons are sure to disappear just as quickly. And what's Passover without matzo *brei*? Our recipe will introduce you to a secret ingredient sure to surprise and delight. If these aren't enough, be sure to check the Take-Along and Comfort Foods chapters for more Passover-approved desserts.

WINE SUGGESTIONS

Moderately Priced Red:
Recanati Yasmine Red (Israel), Kosher

Special-Occasion Red:
Yarden Cabernet Sauvignon (Israel), Kosher

Moderately Priced White:
Recanati Yasmine White (Israel), Kosher

Special-Occasion White:
Goose Bay Sauvignon Blanc (New Zealand)

THE FACTS

1. Passover begins on the fifteenth day of the month of Nissan and lasts for seven or eight days (depending on where you live). It usually falls in early spring.
2. It primarily revolves around the story of the Jews' exodus from Egypt after four hundred years of slavery.
3. We traditionally observe Passover by having a seder, a family meal filled with rituals to remind us of the story of the exodus.
4. A Haggadah is used as the basis for the service during a seder. It tells the story of how God rescued the Israelites from slavery in Egypt and traditionally contains songs, prayers, and narration for those attending the seder. It can be passed on via family, school, or temple or created to fit one's own family needs. (See our Haggadah sidebar for more information on creating your own.)
5. A seder plate should sit on the table and contain: *Maror* (horseradish to represent the bitterness of slavery); *Charoset* (apples, nuts, and cinnamon, a symbol of the maror that slaves used to build Egyptian structures); *Karpas* (often parsley or celery, which is dipped into salt water to represent the tears shed during Egyptian slavery); *Z'roa* (a shank bone, which stands in for the Paschal lamb, a biblical Passover sacrifice); and *Beitzah* (a roasted egg believed to be representative of the festival sacrifice as well as a symbol of mourning for the loss of the temple in Jerusalem). A separate plate containing three pieces of matzo should be on the table, as well as a dish of salt water for dipping the green vegetable. Last, the host should place an extra cup of wine on the table for Elijah.
6. Children play a large role in the Passover seder, and the youngest child often asks the traditional "Four Questions."
7. The *afikomen* is the last piece of food eaten at the seder. It is traditionally hidden for children to find and then "negotiate" for its return.
8. For all of Passover, Jews are forbidden to eat or posses *chametz,* which consists of any wheat, spelt, barley, oats, or rye that has come into contact with water for more than eighteen minutes.

DID YOU KNOW?

- Passover is the oldest continuously celebrated Jewish festival.
- The three pieces of matzo symbolize the three classes of Jewish people in ancient times: the Kohens, the Levites, and the Israelites.
- Both Coke and Pepsi make "kosher for Passover" versions of their sodas.
- One of the most popular Haggadahs in the United States during the beginning of the twentieth century, and the first mass-produced adaptation, was arranged, edited, and translated by a woman named Lillie Cowen.
- Passover's name comes from the last of the ten plagues, in which Jewish homes were "passed over" during the killing of the firstborn male children.
- According to The National Jewish Population Survey (NJPS) 2000–01, 4.3 million of the 5.2 million Jews living in the United States attend a Passover seder.

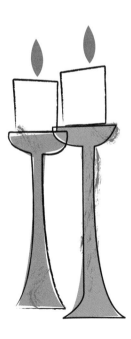

REAL WORLD TRADITIONS

"Instead of a seder, one year my family and I decided to do something a little different . . . so we had a Yiddish lesson. It was hilarious!"

—JILL, NEW YORK CITY, NEW YORK

"My wife and I live far from our families, so my mother makes care packages for the holidays every year. Usually it's overloaded with food, but she looks for weird objects to include. One year for Passover she sent us a box of plush toys representing the icons from the seder—an egg, a lamb shank, etc. . . . "

—SCOTT, HOLLYWOOD, FLORIDA

"Here in Brazil on Easter we have a big thing about chocolate eggs. One month before the holiday all the shops and supermarkets sell a variety of huge chocolate eggs filled with candy, and people give each other those chocolates—it's a big thing for kids. When we were younger, my grandparents used to hide the chocolate eggs on Passover instead of matzo, so we were more motivated to look for it around the house . . . and then after negotiate the afikomen."

—LINA, PORTO ALEGRE, BRAZIL

"Since my niece, Rachel, was about sixteen years old, she has kept a list of everyone who has attended my sister's seder in Kansas City, Missouri. It's in the back of one of the Haggadahs, marked with her name on it. Every year when we go to Kansas City, it's fun to see who is there, who attended last year and the year before that. It's also a time to add the names of husbands and wives and babies, and to see how the family is expanding, as well as to remember those who are no longer with us."

—DEDE, MIAMI, FLORIDA

"My mom goes all out on Passover to help explain the plagues to my nieces through live table theater. I mean, the woman actually buys rubber bugs to signify locusts and throws them on the seder table. Boils are cotton balls with band-aids, and red dye is water turning into blood . . . it's a real treat to see live!"

—STACY, PHILADELPHIA, PENNSYLVANIA

"The first year I lived with my Israeli husband, he came up to me on the first day of Shavuot [a Jewish holiday that follows Passover and commemorates receiving the Torah from God] and cracked an egg on my head! While I was getting over my shock, he explained to me that during Shavuot in Israel, all of the kids run around in the streets and have egg, water balloon, and silly-string fights. Now, when Shavuot rolls around, I always manage to dump some cold water on my hubby's head when he least expects it."

—JULIE, WASHINGTON, D.C.

"I grew up in a household that celebrated all holidays, Jewish and Christian, but was never prone to one or the other until later in life. . . . When I was younger, my mom decided to host Passover and, it being her first time, she was a little nervous. My grandmother brought the brisket and matzo ball soup, and my mother made all of the other preparations for dinner. I was probably about twelve years old at the time and just starting to help my mom with planning and carrying out family functions. As we all know and do at Passover dinner, everyone takes turns reading the traditional stories and prayers associated with Passover. I was asked to read a portion of the reading and, being twelve and a little nervous in front of my family of twenty, reluctantly I agreed. All was going fine with the reading and pronunciation until for some unknown reason instead of saying the word 'Egypt' I said 'Jesus' instead. My grandmother spit out her food and everyone started hysterically laughing. I, of course, was embarrassed and, at the time, they all made me feel fine about it. But there is not a Passover dinner that goes by without my slip being brought up!"

—JAMIE, WEST PALM BEACH, FLORIDA

"My little brother was super-competitive and had a terrible temper, so at every Passover my family would hide TWO afikomen: one for him and one for the rest of us!"

—JODI, RYE BROOK, NEW YORK

CHOPPED LIVER

Roz grew up watching her mother and grandmother grind the liver in a meat grinder that used to screw onto the side of the kitchen table, which is why for many years she bought her chopped liver. With the introduction of the food processor (Cuisinart), there is no excuse to not make it yourself. It really is easy and delicious.

SERVES: 8–10   PREPARATION TIME: 30 MINUTES

6 peeled cold hard-boiled eggs
½ cup vegetable oil
1 large onion, chopped
1 clove garlic, minced
1 pound chicken livers
2 teaspoons salt
1 teaspoon pepper

1. Put the hard-boiled eggs in a food processor and pulse until coarsely chopped. Place in a bowl for later.
2. Heat the oil in a skillet and sauté the onion and garlic until the onion is soft and golden, about 15 minutes.
3. While the onion is cooking, rinse and dry the chicken livers and cut large pieces in half. Add the livers to the onions and continue to sauté until the livers are no longer pink in the middle (about 10 minutes).
4. Transfer the onions, chicken livers, and oil to a bowl to cool for about 20 minutes.
5. Put the chicken livers and onion mixture into the food processor and pulse until pureed.
6. Add the hard-boiled eggs and pulse quickly.
7. Remove the mixture from the processor, put in a bowl, and season with salt and pepper to taste.
8. Refrigerate for at least 2 hours. Serve with sliced cucumber and matzo crackers.

GEFILTE FISH

SERVES: 6

1 24-ounce jar all-white gefilte fish, Manischewitz or Mother's

Serve with mild horseradish, red or white.

Once and for All: The Four Questions

Why does this night differ from all other nights? For on all other nights we eat either leavened or unleavened bread; why on this night only unleavened bread?

On all other nights we eat all kinds of herbs; why on this night only bitter herbs?

On all other nights we need not dip our herbs even once; why on this night must we dip them twice?

On all other nights we eat either sitting up or reclining; why on this night do we all recline?

BABY DAVID'S CHICKEN SOUP WITH WHITE MEATBALLS (MATZO BALLS)

My brother David has quite a way with words. He was also, growing up, a very, very picky eater. The one thing he always loved, though, was a good chicken soup with matzo balls—or to paraphrase his younger self, "white meatballs!"

SERVES: 8–10   PREPARATION TIME: 15 MINUTES
COOKING TIME: 3–3½ HOURS

1–2-pound whole chicken (or cut up)
3 stalks celery with ends cut off
5 peeled carrots
¼ bunch fresh parsley tied together with thread
1 medium onion (you can cut in half to fit better in pot)
3–3½ quarts water (depending on the size of the chicken)
Salt and pepper

1. Clean the chicken (see "Cleaning a Chicken," page 23) and place it in a large (8-quart) soup pot.
2. Add all the other ingredients and cover completely with water.
3. Bring to a gentle boil and simmer for 3 to 3½ hours, or until the soup turns yellow and the chicken starts falling apart.
4. Remove the chicken, parsley, and celery from the soup, but leave the carrots.
5. Season with salt and pepper to taste.
6. Time to make the matzo balls!

MATZO BALLS (AKA WHiTE MEATBALLS)

MAKES: 12 BALLS   PREPARATION TIME: 20 MINUTES
COOKING TIME: 30–40 MINUTES

4 large eggs
½ cup vegetable oil
1 cup matzo meal
½ teaspoon salt

1. In a medium bowl, mix the eggs with vegetable oil.
2. Add the matzo meal and salt, and mix well. Let the mixture stand 15 minutes.
3. In a large pot with a tight-fitting lid, bring 3 to 3½ quarts water to a boil.
4. Using wet hands, form the matzo mixture into balls the size of walnuts.
5. Drop the balls into the boiling water, cover the pot tightly, reduce the heat, and simmer for 30 minutes.
6. Remove the matzo balls with a slotted spoon and add to the warm chicken soup.

✱ If you want to prepare this dish a day or two ahead of time, add the matzo balls to the soup before refrigerating. By sitting in the soup, the matzo balls will take on the taste of the broth. When your guests arrive, simply remove from the fridge and reheat.

CHAROSET

This is a simple traditional recipe for charoset. Make it at least a day ahead of time so that the apples soak up the honey and wine.

SERVES: 8   PREPARATION TIME: 30 MINUTES
REFRIGERATE FOR AT LEAST 4–5 HOURS, PREFERABLY OVERNIGHT

10 peeled, cored and chopped apples (Gala, Red Delicious, or Fuji)
1¼ cups chopped walnuts
12 tablespoons honey
2½ teaspoons cinnamon
Mogan David grape wine to taste (⅛–¼ cup)

Mix all ingredients together and refrigerate for a minimum of 4 to 5 hours.

✳ When serving, put the charoset into three or four different bowls up and down the table for easy access, as everyone seems to eat it throughout the seder and the meal.

Creating Your Own Haggadah

Roz's husband (and Andrea's father), Allan, is usually handed the daunting task of leading the Passover seder. After years of trial and error, he has finally come up with a workable strategy for creating a family Haggadah. We asked him to share his knowledge.

"Whoever enlarges on the telling of the Exodus is praiseworthy."

Among all the Jewish holidays, none has a greater direct relationship to food than Passover. In fact, the central fixture of the Passover table is a seder plate containing specific foods that are consumed for the sole purpose of identifying with the Exodus of the Jews from their slavery in Egypt.

Parsley, one of the bitter herbs on the seder plate, represents the bitterness of slavery, while the salt water represents the tears shed by the Jews while in bondage in Egypt. The foods on the seder plate are physically joined with each diner by their consumption during the retelling of the Exodus in the Haggadah. Haggadah actually means "telling" and is a fulfillment of the scriptural commandment to each Jew to "tell your son" about the Jewish liberation from slavery in Egypt, as described in the book of Exodus in the Torah. (Next time you watch *The Ten Commandments,* there is a scene about ninety seconds long in which Moses, portrayed by Charlton Heston, performs a small portion of the seder before he leads the Hebrews to freedom.)

While the Haggadah is designed to be a "narrative," very little of the classic Haggadah is devoted to a simple telling of the Exodus story. Instead, the rabbis wove a variety of activities into the seder event that purportedly serve to highlight the values of the Exodus and enable the participants to "learn by doing." Presently more than three thousand known editions of the Haggadah exist, and in recent years a new effort has begun to express the story of the Passover in contemporary terms and with allusions to current struggles. There have been many textual additions to the

Haggadah as well as commentaries on the meaning of the texts and actions over the ages; still, a basic structure (seder means "order") remains.

Therein lies the rub. It is unusual to find a Jew who cannot recount at least one seder, normally experienced as a child, as "taking forever before we finally ate." The reality is that a seder can last as long as several hours and can be as short as thirty minutes. The length of the "telling" is normally a function of the length of the Haggadah. Our own experience has been instructive and may assist you in determining how to "tell" of the Exodus.

When we were first married we would normally celebrate Passover at Roz's parents' home, and the full-length Haggadah was the operative version. Normally, somewhere between sixty and ninety minutes were dedicated to the "telling" before we could begin the "festive meal." The unspoken irony was that there were initially no children at the seder and all the participants had been "told" the story many times before. These seders tended to focus on the prayers and songs, sometimes at the expense of the drama associated with the story of delivery from bondage. This same seder was repeated for many years, despite the fact that the numbers of those sons (and daughters) to be "told" were expanding.

As we became the "tellers" of the story, we decided to try some alternatives. One year we focused almost exclusively on the content and meaning of the seder plate. I located a wonderful Web site, The Virtual Seder Plate, and I printed out the explanation of each part of the seder plate. I distributed a section to some of our family and guests, which they read aloud. We learned quite a bit about the objects associated with a religious observance we had witnessed or performed many, many times before. We did "tell" the story, but on that particular night we focused on the symbolic nature of each item. It was a great way to celebrate Passover, and we have done it again on more than one occasion. On another Passover I had just finished reading *Mystic Quest: An Introduction to Jewish Mysticism,* by David Ariel, and we incorporated some aspects of Kabbalah into our seder.

As our children grew older and we were blessed with the arrival of our own grandchildren, we finally put our gelt where our mouths were and created our own Haggadah. As with most things that are on one's lifetime "to-do" list, the anticipation was much more difficult than the doing. We made a decision to "tell" the story of the Exodus with more emphasis on the "why" and not the "what." If you have the desire to make your own Haggadah, the basic outline (which we have provided below), an older Haggadah that is comprehensive, and access to a computer, you will find that by dedicating a few hours an evening over the course of a week, you will have become "praiseworthy." Begin with the understanding that the seder and the Haggadah consist of the following segments:

Sanctifying the holiday;
Washing the hands;
Eating the green vegetable dipped in
    salt water;
Breaking the middle matzo;
Reciting the narrative;
Washing the hands (before eating
    the meal);
Blessing for the bread and the matzo;
Eating the bitter herb;
Eating the matzah with the bitter herb;
Eating the meal;
Finding the afikomen;
Reciting the grace after meals;
Singing Psalms of praise; and
Concluding with the hope that the Exodus
has been told with the appropriate intention.

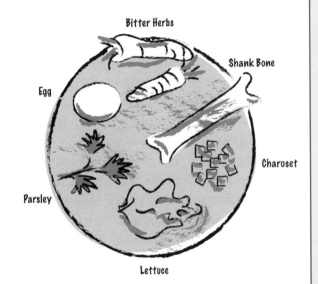

After that, it is totally in your hands. I used normal search engines and simple search terms on Google to find more resource information than I ultimately needed to create precisely what we wanted. I would strongly suggest that when you are creating your own Haggadah, you consider the anticipated changes in the size of your family (the new members, the relative attention span of all members); their general personal religious convictions; and their ability to become an unruly mob. Armed with this knowledge, create your Haggadah with sections that can be utilized or passed over (no pun intended) at any particular seder. Keep in mind who you are "telling" the story of Exodus to. Don't lose sight of the scriptural commandment in favor of scripture. There are a number of Web sites with a lot of Judaic clip-art on the Internet (some free) that can make your personal Haggadah more pleasing to the eye and interesting for the younger participants.

If you use your computer and some simple search terms, there are innumerable Web sites that have a lot of information about the Passover holiday. Most of them also make great suggestions for including young children in the seder (for example, when telling of the plagues that befell the Egyptians, get some plastic animals to portray the frogs and beasts; ping-pong balls or plastic golf balls for hail; red food coloring for blood, and so on).

Having had this experience, I strongly encourage you to create your own Haggadah at the time best suited to you and your family. By the way, at the end don't forget to include the phrase "*Shulchan Orech*" or "The Festive Meal." Hopefully it will become for you, as it has for our family, the segue from your "telling" to a wonderful family meal with the incredible food found in this book.

BROCCOLI SOUFFLÉ

It may not be the healthiest option on the table, but it's certainly the tastiest (in Andrea's humble opinion). This soufflé is also a great vegetarian option—it's savory and filling, and even better reheated with leftovers the next day.

SERVES: 6–8   PREPARATION TIME: 15–20 MINUTES
COOKING TIME: 35 MINUTES

2 10-ounce packages frozen broccoli
1 cup mayonnaise (I prefer Hellmann's)
1 10¾-ounce can cream of mushroom soup
1 tablespoon apple cider vinegar
2 eggs, well beaten
1 8-ounce package shredded cheddar cheese

1. Preheat the oven to 350°F.
2. Cook the broccoli per instructions on the box and drain well.
3. Grease a 1½- to 2-quart casserole dish with cooking spray.
4. Mix all of the ingredients together and pour into the casserole dish.
5. Bake for 35 minutes. Casserole will be lightly browned and firm to the touch.

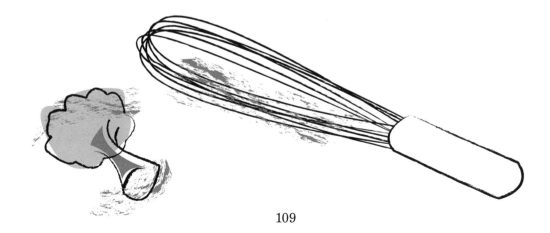

ROAST TURKEY

Most everyone knows how to roast a turkey, but not necessarily how to make a moist and juicy one. After years of trial and error, and many dry turkeys, we have found a way that seems to work every time. The secret is roasting the turkey with the breast side down and making sure there is always chicken broth in the bottom of the pan. We flip the turkey for the last 45 minutes to crisp the skin, but baste the breast side every 15 minutes as well.

SERVES: UP TO 15–18   PREPARATION TIME: 30 MINUTES
COOKING TIME: APPROXIMATELY 3–4 HOURS

12-pound turkey
1 stick margarine
Salt
Pepper
Garlic salt
1 16-ounce box chicken broth

1. Preheat the oven to 325°F.
2. Rinse and dry the turkey. Slice half of the margarine into 5 or 6 pieces; let the rest soften.
3. Carefully tuck the slices of margarine under the skin of the turkey, pushing them back near the large breast area. (Be very gentle, as you don't want to tear the skin.)
4. Sprinkle the turkey with salt, pepper, and garlic salt.
5. Pour half of the chicken broth into the bottom of the roasting pan.
6. Place the turkey in the pan, breast-side down.
7. Roast the turkey for 15 to 20 minutes per pound.
8. For the last 45 minutes, turn the turkey breast-side up to brown the top, basting every 15 to 20 minutes. If breast area begins to get too brown, cover the turkey with foil. Continue to add broth to the bottom of the pan, making sure it is never dry.

✳ Let the turkey sit for at least 30 minutes before slicing. Add salt and pepper to taste if needed.

✳ For gravy, simply use the juices at the bottom of the roasting pan. Just put the juices in a pot, skim off excess grease, and reheat on top of the stove when ready to serve.

The Burning Question: Everything You Ever Wanted to Know about Matzo

It's no secret that matzo is far from most people's favorite food—especially once you hit the third or fourth day—but how bad is matzo for you nutritionally? We asked Mandi Pek (M.S., R.D., C.S.P., C.D.N., and friend of Andrea) and got the facts.

On a scale of 1 to 10, how nutritious is matzo?
One sheet of matzo has about the same nutritional value as a slice and a half of bread. Matzo can fit into a healthy Passover diet, but the cardboard has calories. On its own, it's probably about a 2.

Any dietary issues with eating matzo for eight days?
Yes! Matzo can cause constipation. To help avoid this, it's really important to make sure that you are drinking a lot of water. Aim for eight 8-ounce glasses a day. Avoid beverages that dehydrate you like alcohol and caffeine.

It is also very important that you eat more fiber. In general we need 25 to 30 grams of fiber a day. However, if you're eating a lot of matzo, up to 38 grams of fiber a day may be helpful. Be sure to add fiber slowly into your diet to avoid abdominal pain and bloating. Insoluble fiber can be found in many foods including avocados, whole grains, apples with the skin, beans, and many other fruits and veggies.

Any benefit to specific kinds of matzo such as thin tea, whole wheat, egg, or plain matzo?
All of the different types of matzo provide approximately the same number of calories per board, usually between 80 and 110 calories per serving. Some brands of egg matzo are slightly higher in fat. Some brands of whole wheat have more fiber than plain matzo. It seems to be brand specific, so it's important to read the nutrition label on the box and look for at least 3 grams of fiber per serving.

Any benefit to cooking with matzo meal over eating plain matzo?
Matzo meal is just ground up matzo. So the amount you use and what you cook would determine whether or not it is healthier than plain matzo. For example, matzo balls and matzo brei using matzo meal can vary tremendously in the number of calories per serving depending on how they were cooked. Matzo brei are usually made with eggs and oil and then fried. This can make for a very high-calorie meal. Using cooking spray and egg whites can help to decrease the number of calories per serving.

What can we add to or put on matzo to offset the heaviness and help with digestion?
During Passover what we put on our matzo is often more calorically dense then the matzo itself. We tend to add things like cream cheese, butter, peanut butter, or cheese, all of which are high in calories and fat. Adding turkey breast, roast beef, or low-fat tuna would be a better option. Add a side salad with kidney beans and avocado to increase your fiber and help prevent constipation.

What kinds of foods should we add to our diet during Passover to keep things more balanced?
Passover is a perfect time to start eating healthier. Enjoy salads with grilled chicken and a small piece of matzo on the side, or have some low-fat cottage cheese and a sliced apple. Whether it's Passover or any other time of the year, every meal should contain protein, fat, and carbohydrates. Using matzo as a side, like you would a dinner roll, rather than as the main focus of the meal should help prevent stomach upset from this very binding holiday. And always remember to drink plenty of fluids!

PASSOVER ROLLS

These rolls are a real Passover favorite. They taste amazingly bread-like and are a welcome respite from matzo overload. Aside from dinner, they are a great way to make sandwiches during Passover.

SERVES: 6–8   PREPARATION TIME: 20 MINUTES
COOKING TIME: 50 MINUTES

2 cups matzo meal
1 teaspoon salt
1 tablespoon sugar
½ cup peanut oil or vegetable oil
1 cup water
4 eggs

1. Preheat the oven to 375°F.
2. Mix the matzo meal, salt, and sugar.
3. Pour the oil into a saucepan with the water and bring to a boil, then pour over the matzo-meal mixture and mix well.
4. Add the eggs, one at a time, mixing well after each.
5. Let the mixture stand for 15 minutes.
6. Oil your hands and form the dough into balls. Place them on greased baking sheet (use oil or cooking spray).
7. Bake the rolls for 50 minutes.

✳ These are delicious when warmed in the oven just before serving.

✳ The rolls will keep well for 2 days in a sealed baggie.

RED POTATOES

Who doesn't like buttered potatoes? The petite reds look pretty as well in a bowl or on a platter.

SERVES: 8–10 PEOPLE   PREPARATION TIME: 5–10 MINUTES
COOKING TIME: 15 MINUTES

3 pounds petite red potatoes
4 tablespoons butter or margarine
Salt and pepper to taste
Parsley flakes

1. Rinse the potatoes but do not peel them, and put them in a large pot.
2. Fill the pot with enough cold water to cover the potatoes.
3. Bring to a boil and simmer for 12 to 15 minutes; the potatoes should be tender but not mushy when pricked with a fork.
4. Drain well.
5. Add the butter, salt, and pepper to taste.
6. Mix the potatoes gently so all are coated with the butter.
7. Sprinkle lightly with parsley flakes and serve.

✳ Use leftovers for hash browns the next night—delicious! (Dice an onion and cut up the potatoes; add 2 tablespoons butter or margarine, and brown to crisp.)

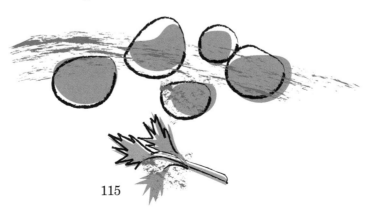

SWEET SALAD DRESSING

This dressing is sweet and tangy. It really adds a little kick to the meal.

MAKES: ABOUT 3 CUPS, SERVES 24

1 cup red wine vinegar
2 cups vegetable oil
10 tablespoons sugar
1 clove garlic, peeled and minced
1¼ teaspoons Dijon mustard
Juice of ¼ lemon
1¼ teaspoons black pepper
¼ cup dried cranberries (Craisins)
½ cup bleu cheese or feta

1. Combine all ingredients in a jar or pitcher.
2. Serve over a tossed salad with cucumbers, red and yellow peppers, tomatoes, romaine and iceberg lettuce.

✳ For a more traditional taste, leave out the dried cranberries and cheese.

✳ The dressing will keep in the fridge for a week.

PASSOVER BROWNiES

Passover desserts, especially chocolate ones that are good, are hard to find. These brownies are some of the best we've had.

SERVES: 6–8   PREPARATION TIME: 15–20 MINUTES
COOKING TIME: 30–35 MINUTES

4 eggs
2 cups sugar
½ cup unsweetened cocoa
1 cup oil
½ teaspoon salt
1 cup Passover cake meal
1 cup chopped walnuts
2 cups chocolate chips

1. Preheat the oven to 325°F.
2. Beat the eggs and sugar well. Add the cocoa, oil, and salt and mix until thoroughly combined.
3. Gradually add the cake meal, nuts, and chocolate chips.
4. Coat a 9 x 13-inch baking pan with cooking spray and pour the batter into the greased pan.
5. Bake for 30 to 35 minutes.
6. Cool the brownies and cut into squares.
7. Sprinkle with powdered sugar or regular granulated sugar.

AUNT FRIEDA'S NUT CAKE

Roz's Aunt Frieda always made this cake for Passover, and Roz looked forward to it every year—even freezing leftover pieces. For some reason no one in our family writes down their recipes (until now!), but one of the last times Frieda made the cake Roz's mom, Edith, wrote down everything so she could pass it along to us. It's so good you really could make it all year long.

SERVES: 8–10 PREPARATION TIME: 45–50 MINUTES
COOKING TIME: 1 HOUR

CAKE
2 eggs
2 cups sugar
1 pound ground pecans
¼ cup Passover cake meal
2 lemons, juice and zest

1. Preheat the oven to 350°F.
2. Grease a 10-inch diameter springform pan.
3. Separate the eggs. Beat the egg yolks until frothy. Add the sugar and beat well.
4. Add the pecans and the cake meal. Stir in the lemon juice and zest.
5. Beat the egg whites until stiff and fold them into the batter.
6. Pour the cake batter into the springform pan.
7. Bake for 1 hour.
8. Cool the cake completely and then frost with Chocolate Fudge Icing.
9. Refrigerate the cake for several hours before serving (it's really best if made a day ahead of time).

✳ Place the cake in the fridge to cool faster before icing.

CHOCOLATE FUDGE ICING

½ cup butter or margarine
½ cup unsweetened cocoa
⅓ cup milk
1 16-ounce box confectioners' sugar
1 teaspoon vanilla

1. Melt the butter in a microwave (1 minute).
2. Stir in the cocoa until smooth, then microwave until the mixture boils (around 1 minute).
3. Add the milk, vanilla, and confectioners' sugar, and beat until blended well.
4. Spread the icing over the nut cake.

* The cake freezes very well. After cooling it completely in the refrigerator so the icing hardens, wrap the cake in waxed paper and then again in aluminum foil and place in the freezer. The waxed paper will keep the icing from sticking to the foil.

ALMOND MACAROONS

Anyone who loves almond macaroons will be making these by the dozens. They are easy to make and better than any you can buy at a bakery. Plus they are a lot cheaper to make than to buy!

MAKES: ABOUT A DOZEN PREPARATION TIME: 20 MINUTES
COOKING TIME: 16 MINUTES PER BATCH

1¼ cups almonds
¾ cup sugar
1 egg white
½ teaspoon vanilla extract

1. Preheat the oven to 400°F.
2. Put the almonds and sugar into a food processor with a metal blade. Process just until the mixture is smooth (don't over process).
3. Add 1 egg white and pulse 10 times.
4. Add the vanilla and pulse 2 to 3 times.
5. You should be able to shape the batter with your hands; it should be sticky and thick.
6. Lay a piece of baker's parchment on a baking sheet.
7. Shape the batter into balls the size of walnuts, and arrange them on the parchment.
8. Brush each macaroon with a little water.
9. Bake the macaroons for 16 minutes or until lightly browned.
10. Remove the baking sheet from the oven, cool the cookies completely on the parchment, and remove.
11. Store in a tightly covered container. They also freeze well.

✱ The size of the egg and the amount of oil in the almonds determine the consistency, so you might have to add a bit more ground almonds to make it thicker or egg white if it's too dry to form into a ball.

MATZO BREi

Possibly one of our favorite things to make during Passover, matzo brei works well for breakfast, lunch, or dinner. Though many matzo brei recipes use sugar or call for egg-dipped matzo that are fried, Grandma Edith's recipe throws in some cottage cheese to thicken the mixture and make them more pancake-like. Trust us, they are delicious!

SERVES: 2–3   PREPARATION TIME: 15–20 MINUTES
COOKING TIME: 15 MINUTES

3 matzo squares
2 eggs, lightly beaten
1 cup small-curd cottage cheese
1 tablespoon grated onion or dried minced onion (optional)
½ teaspoon salt
¼ teaspoon pepper
Vegetable oil

1. Break the matzo into pieces and put them in a colander. Run hot water over the matzo to soften them (about 1 minute)
2. Once softened, place the matzo in a large mixing bowl and add the eggs, cottage cheese, onion, and salt and pepper to taste. Mix well.
3. On medium high, heat enough oil in a frying pan to cover the bottom. Drop large spoonfuls of the mixture one at a time into the hot oil. They should be far enough apart that they do not touch.
4. Fry the brei until browned on both sides.

✳ If you want to use only egg whites, substitute 4 whites instead of 2 whole eggs.

✳ You can also replace the oil with cooking spray, though the brei may not be as crispy.

SING!
A Few of Our Favorite Seder Songs

"The Ballad of the Four Sons"
(to the tune of "Clementine")

This one is a classic in the Marks family. Not a seder goes by that we don't sing at least a few of the verses.

Said the father to his children,
"At the seder you will dine,
You will eat your fill of matzah,
You will drink four cups of wine."

Now this father had no daughters,
But his sons they numbered four.
One was wise and one was wicked,
One was simple and a bore.

And the fourth was sweet and winsome,
he was young and he was small.
While his brothers asked the questions
he could scarcely speak at all.

Said the wise one to his father,
"Would you please explain the laws?
Of the customs of the seder
Will you please explain the cause?"

And the father proudly answered,
"As our fathers ate in speed,

Ate the paschal lamb 'ere midnight
And from slavery were freed."

So we follow their example
And 'ere midnight must complete
All the seder and we should not
After twelve remain to eat.

Then did sneer the son so wicked,
"What does all this mean to you?"
And the father's voice was bitter
As his grief and anger grew.

"If you yourself don't consider
As son of Israel,
Then for you this has no meaning
You could be a slave as well."

Then the simple son said simply,
"What is this," and quietly
The good father told his offspring,
"We were freed from slavery."

But the youngest son was silent
For he could not ask at all.
His bright eyes were bright with wonder
As his father told him all.

My dear children, heed the lesson
and remember evermore
What the father told his children
Told his sons that numbered four.

"Dayenu"

Perhaps the most famous of all Passover songs (and Roz's favorite), "Dayenu" (which means "it would have been enough") is over a thousand years old and actually has fifteen stanzas, signifying the fifteen gifts that God bestowed on the Jews. We give you three.

Ilu hotzi, hotzianu
Hotzianu miMitzrayim
Hotzianu miMitzrayim
Dayenu.

(Chorus)
Day, day, yenu
Day, day, yenu
Day, day, yenu
Dayenu dayenu.

Ilu natan natan lanu
Natan lanu et haShabbat
Natan lanu et haShabbat
Dayenu.

(Chorus)

Ilu natan natan lanu
Natan lanu et haTorah
Natan lanu et haTorah
Dayenu.

(Chorus)

"Let My People Go"

A song not only familiar to seder-goers, but to Ferris Bueller fans as well.

When Israel was in Egypt land
Let my people go
Oppressed so hard they could not
stand
Let my people go.

(Chorus)
Go down Moses,
Way down to Egypt land
Tell old Pharoah
To let my people go.

And God told Moses what to do
Let my people go!
To lead the children of Israel through
Let my people go!

(Chorus)

"The Four Questions"

Anyone who made it through years of Hebrew school will recognize this tune. It is a lovely song and an easy way to introduce younger children to the Four Questions.

Mah nishtahnah haLailah hazeh
Mi kol ha lailot
Mi kol ha lailot
Sheh b'chol halailot
anu ochlin
chametz u'matzh
chametz u'matzh
HaLailah hazeh
HaLailah hazeh
kulo matzah,
HaLailah hazeh
kulo matzah.

Sheh b'chol haLailot
anu ochlin
She'ar yirakot
She'ar yirakot
HaLailah hazeh
HaLailah hazeh
Maror.
HaLailah hazeh
Maror.

Sheh b'chol haLailot
ein anu matbilin
Afilu pa'am ehad
Afilu pa'am ehad)
HaLailah hazeh
HaLailah hazeh
Sh'tei f'amim,
HaLailah hazeh
Sh'tei f'amim.

Sheh b'chol haLailot
Anu oclin
Bein yoshvin
u'vein m'subin
u'vein m'subin
HaLailah hazeh
HaLailah hazeh
Kulanu m'subin.
HaLailah hazeh
Kulanu m'subin.

A FEW MORE JEWISH HOLIDAYS

Obviously, Judaism consists of much more than the holidays mentioned thus far in this book. There is an entire calendar full of holidays that, unfortunately, we weren't able to cover in depth (hello, sequel!). Below we've given you a brief overview of some other major holidays on the Jewish calendar, along with some fun facts and tips for celebrating.

SUKKOT

Sukkot falls immediately after Yom Kippur and, though following one of the most serious and solemn holidays, is all about rejoicing. In fact, it is often referred to as the "Season of our Rejoicing," or *Z'man Simchateinu*. The idea behind the celebration is one part historical and one part agricultural, as it not only commemorates the years spent wandering in the desert but also acts as a harvest festival. Below are a few fast facts about Sukkot:

- Sukkot means "booths," and refers to the temporary shelters Jews were commanded to live in during their period of wandering.
- A main part of the holiday revolves around building and decorating a *sukkah* (great fun for the kids!) with everything from fruits and vegetables (usually dried squash and corn) to children's artwork.
- A sukkah must have at least two-and-a-half walls covered with material that will not blow away in the wind, and a roof made from *sekhakh* (meaning "covering"). The sekhakh needs to be something that came from the ground (such as branches, cornstalks, bamboo, etc.). The sekhakh should be left loose and be sparse enough that rain can get through but not sparse enough that there is more light than shade.
- Observant Jews are encouraged to spend as much time as possible in the sukkah (including sleeping in it!), but the idea of "dwelling" in the sukkah can be simply eating all of one's meals inside it.
- It's no coincidence that Sukkot is reminiscent of Thanksgiving. Some believe that the Pilgrims based the holiday on Sukkot.

- Another major observance is the use of the *lulav* and *etrog.* The lulav consists of a palm branch, two willow branches, and three myrtle branches. The etrog is a citrus fruit similar to a lemon and is native to Israel. Holding each in one hand, they are brought together and are waved in six directions (north, south, east, west, up, and down) to recognize that God is everywhere.

- One of the most interesting traditions of Sukkot (at least in our opinion) is that of the *Ushpizin,* or Seven Guests. For each of the seven nights of the holiday, Jews are encouraged to "invite" leaders of historical importance to join them in the sukkah. The traditional invitees are Abraham, Isaac, Jacob, Joseph, Moses, Aaron, and David, and they are considered, for the night, to be the most honored guest.

SIMCHAT TORAH

Simchat Torah follows Sukkot on the Jewish calendar as another celebratory holiday. Each week in temple, Jews read passages from the Torah, starting with Genesis and ending with Deuteronomy. Simchat Torah celebrates the reading of the last chapter, which is then immediately followed by Genesis once again. It reminds congregants that the Torah is never-ending. A few more facts:

- The holiday is observed with a fun, high-spirited celebration. The ark that houses the Torahs is opened, all the Torahs are removed, and the congregants participate in a processional around the synagogue filled with dancing, singing, and prayers.
- As many people as possible are called for an *aliyah,* or blessing over the Torah reading, even children who are normally too young to receive one.
- Simchat Torah is a wonderful family holiday, as children are encouraged to run around with small (sometimes plush) Torahs in the synagogue and general craziness is accepted.
- Drinking is not uncommon during this holiday; aside from Purim, it is the holiday most associated with alcohol according to most texts.

TU B'SHEVAT

Anyone who ever made his or her way through Jewish day school (or Hebrew school, for that matter) knows this holiday as the "tree holiday," and that's precisely what it is: a New Year's for Trees. It acts as a specific date to calculate the age of trees, as the Torah states that the fruit of the trees cannot be eaten for the first three years and the fourth year the fruit is reserved for God. More facts:

- Many celebrate this holiday by planting a tree, eating a new fruit, or collecting money to plant trees in Israel.
- It is customary to eat fruits that remind us of Israel including grapes, olives, dates, figs, and pomegranates. The blessing over fruit is said: *Baruch atah A-donoy, Elo-heinu Melech Ha'Olam borei pri ha-aitz;* Blessed are You, Lord our God, King of the universe, who creates the fruit of the tree.

PURIM

Purim is truly a holiday of fun and celebration. It is based around the Book of Esther (or Megillah Esther) and tells the story of how the Jewish people were delivered from the ancient Persian empire when King Ahausuerus's royal advisor, Haman, planned to massacre them. In the story, the beautiful Esther becomes queen, though the King does not know that she is a Jew. Upon the advice of her cousin Mordecai, she approaches the King (a dangerous act) and tells him of Haman's plot against her people, thus saving the Jews from extermination. More facts:

- The Book of Esther is believed to be the only book of the Bible that does not contain the name of God. In fact, there is little or no reference to God at all.
- It is celebrated on the fourteenth day of Adar (usually falling in March), the day the Jews celebrated their survival.
- The holiday is preceded by The Fast of Esther, in which we commemorate Esther's three-day fast prior to meeting with the King.
- During the reading of the Megillah it is customary to shout, boo, stomp, and shake noise-makers when the name "Haman" is mentioned.
- On Purim, drinking is encouraged. In fact, there are many conflicting opinions on just how drunk one is commanded to get on the holiday . . . but we'll leave that up to your own research and good judgment!
- Jews are also commanded to send food and gifts and to make gifts to charity. The custom is known as *Matanot LaEvyonim,* and specifies that a minimum of two gifts be given to people in need. The gift should be given during the day and can come either directly or through a third party.
- It is customary to hold celebrations, perform plays, and dress up as characters from the story of Purim.
- The Jewish women's organization Hadassah was named for Queen Esther when it was founded in 1912, as Hadassah is Hebrew for Esther.

THE NEW, OLD-FASHIONED HAMANTASCHEN

Hamantaschen are the traditional pastry of Purim. Their three-sided shape is sometimes
thought to be modeled on Haman's hat and even has a song associated with it:
My hat it has three corners. Three corners has my hat. And had it not three corners,
It wouldn't be my hat. Clever, no? This recipe comes courtesy of my very good friend, the lovely
Deborah Edell, owner of Perry Street Cakes in New York City.

SERVES: 8–10
PREPARATION TIME: ABOUT ½ HOUR PLUS 2 HOURS TO CHILL THE DOUGH
COOKING TIME: 20–25 MINUTES PER BATCH

3 cups all-purpose flour, sifted

1½ teaspoons baking powder

¼ teaspoon salt

10 tablespoons unsalted butter (1¼ sticks), room temperature

½ cup sugar

1 large egg

3 tablespoons orange juice

½ teaspoon vanilla

1 jar strawberry preserves

1. In a medium bowl, whisk together the flour, baking powder, and salt. Set aside. In a large
   mixing bowl, beat the butter until smooth. Add the sugar and beat until fluffy. Add the egg
   and beat until just incorporated.
2. Add the juice and vanilla. Beat until smooth.
3. Gradually add the flour mixture until well incorporated. You may wish to transfer the
   dough to a floured surface and knead it until smooth, but this is not necessary.
4. Divide the dough into 2 balls and wrap in plastic. Refrigerate for at least 2 hours.
5. Preheat the oven to 350°F. Lightly grease two cookie sheets, so you can prepare one while
   the other bakes.

6. Remove one of the balls of dough from the fridge and roll out on a lightly floured surface with a rolling pin to about ⅛ inch thick. (Or you can roll out the dough between two sheets of plastic.) Using a 3-inch round cookie cutter or the rim of a drinking glass, cut out rounds. Re-roll any scraps.

7. Spoon a heaping teaspoon full of jam into the center of each round of pastry. Using your fingers, pinch the edges of the dough together around the filling to form a triangle. Pinch the edges tightly at each corner so that the filling stays in the cookie.

8. Place the hamantaschen about 1 inch apart on the cookie sheets.

9. Bake for about 20 to 25 minutes or until very lightly brown or golden. Cool them on the sheets 5 minutes and then move to wire racks to cool completely.

10. Repeat with the remaining dough until all the cookies are baked.

KOSHER CAIPIRINHA

Purim is a celebration and, trust us, no one knows how to celebrate like Brazilians. In fact, Purim has been compared to both Mardi Gras and Brazil's Carnaval for its festivities and joyous celebration. So, in the spirit of our Jewish-Brazilian family (see the Carneiro side), we present a Purim cocktail that is guaranteed to inspire good times. Just be careful and responsible, Cachaça is not for the lightweight drinker! Seriously. (Warning: To incorporate her husband's background into an otherwise traditional Jewish ceremony, Andrea and Gil served these delicious drinks to a restaurant full of non-Brazilians at their wedding. Chaos ensued.)

MAKES: 1 DRINK

1 lime
4 teaspoons sugar (or 2½ packets Splenda or other artificial sweetener)
1 ounce kosher Cachaça (or kosher vodka)
Ice cubes

1. Cut the lime in half lengthwise and squeeze the juice from each half into a glass, using a lime squeezer.
2. Take the remnants of the lime and cut each side in half and then into thirds, and add them to the glass.
3. Add the sugar (or Splenda). You can add more or less sugar depending on personal preference.
4. Use a masher or wooden spoon to mash the sugar into the lime wedges as you stir.
5. Eyeball the amount of liquid now in the glass, and add a little less Cachaça than that amount.
6. Use your masher to continue mashing the ingredients while stirring.
7. Fill the glass with ice and let the drink sit for a few minutes to chill.

✳ You can use anything from a tumbler to a highball to a goblet to make this drink, but be sure your glass has a thick bottom and plenty of room for ice.

✳ Caipirinhas (and Caipiroskas) are best when very cold, so as your ice melts, continue to add more ice to keep your drink cold.

✳ You can substitute kosher vodka for Cachaça if you like, and the Caipirinha becomes a Caipiroska!

TAKE-ALONG FOODS

"Food is an important part of a balanced diet."

—FRAN LEBOWITZ

Sometimes we don't have the time or the energy (or the space!) to host a crowd for dinner. In those times we give thanks for friends, family . . . and even in-laws. But in the grand tradition of Judaism there can never be too much food. Hence we give you the Take-Along. Mostly consisting of desserts (though we did throw in a few sides), these recipes are delicious, simple, and best of all, easily transportable. Whether a traditional raisin kugel, or the Markses' favorite orange cake, we promise you'll be lauded as a great guest . . . and a great cook!

CHOCOLATE-COVERED PRETZELS AND CHOCOLATE-COVERED STRAWBERRiES

We love our daughter-in-law/sister-in-law Sarah's Grandma Marilyn for many reasons: her fabulous baby blankets, her embarrassing stories about Sarah, and her willingness to accept the insanity that is the Marks family and still visit us for holidays. But one of the most wonderful things about Grandma Marilyn's visits is her fantastic chocolate-covered strawberries and chocolate-covered pretzels. In fact, sometimes it can get quite ugly when it comes to divvying up the leftovers at the end of the night. We asked her to donate this recipe and were shocked at how easy it is to make. These two desserts are not only easily transportable, but will leave your hosts wondering just how you found the time to make such a fabulous dessert!

SERVES: 10–12   PREPARATION TIME: 5 MINUTES
COOKING TIME: 15 MINUTES

1 16-ounce box Eagle Brand Chocolate Candy Coating
1 16-ounce box Eagle Brand White Chocolate Candy Coating
1 pint fresh strawberries, rinsed and dried, with the hulls on
1 16-ounce package mini-salted pretzels or home-style pretzels

1. Put the chocolate candy coating in one saucepan and the white chocolate in another saucepan over low heat and melt but do not bring to a boil.
2. Line two cookie sheets with waxed paper.

CHOCOLATE STRAWBERRiES

When the chocolates are melted, carefully dip the top third of each of the strawberries, one at a time, into the chocolate and place on one of the cookie sheets to cool. Dip some strawberries in the white chocolate and some in the plain chocolate. When finished with the strawberries, place them in the refrigerator until you are ready to serve them or to take them to someone's house. They should be transported on a flat serving dish.

CHOCOLATE PRETZELS

Take a few pretzels at a time and drop them in the chocolates. Pull them out when covered and place them on a cookie sheet to cool. Put them in the refrigerator for about 30 minutes to harden. Once they are hardened, you can transfer them into any container you like. They won't melt or stick together.

APPLE-RAISIN NOODLE KUGEL

There are numerous sweet noodle kugel recipes, and here is one of our favorites.
How bad can noodles, ricotta, sour cream, sugar, and raisins be?

SERVES: 10–12   PREPARATION TIME: 20 MINUTES
COOKING TIME: 45–55 MINUTES

1 tablespoon butter
12-ounce package egg noodles
2 cups part-skim ricotta cheese
1 cup sour cream
5 eggs
½ cup skim milk
½ cup sugar
1 tablespoon vanilla
2 teaspoons cinnamon
½ cup golden raisins (or black raisins)
2 apples, peeled and cut in small pieces
½ stick butter, melted

1. Preheat the oven to 325°F.
2. Grease a 9 x 13-inch glass baking dish with the butter.
3. Cook the noodles according to the instructions on the package and drain them well.
4. In a mixing bowl, whisk together the ricotta, sour cream, and eggs until smooth.
5. Stir in the milk, sugar, vanilla, cinnamon, raisins, and apples.
6. Add the cooked, drained noodles along with the melted butter. Mix well.
7. Pour the mixture into the baking dish.
8. Bake for 45 to 55 minutes or until the kugel is set and golden brown on top.

CARROT TZIMMIS

For the carrot lover, this side dish is a great addition to any meal, with any crowd.

SERVES: 6–8   PREPARATION TIME: 20–25 MINUTES
COOKING TIME: 25 MINUTES

8 medium carrots
2 cups cold water
3 tablespoons butter or margarine
½ teaspoon cinnamon
⅛ teaspoon ground cloves
½ teaspoon salt
¼ cup brown sugar (light or dark)
¼ cup raisins
¼ cup lemon juice
⅛ cup Madeira wine

1. Preheat the oven to 325°F.
2. Peel and cut the carrots into bite-sized chunks.
3. Place the carrots in a saucepan with the cold water and bring to a boil, then cover and simmer until tender (about 10 to 15 minutes)
4. Drain the carrots, reserving 1 cup of the liquid. Put the carrots in a bowl.
5. In the saucepan melt the butter; add the carrot liquid, and stir.
6. Remove the pot from the heat and add the cinnamon, cloves, salt, brown sugar, raisins, lemon juice, and wine. Mix well, then add the carrots and gently stir.
7. Grease a 1½-quart casserole dish (using butter or cooking spray) and pour in the carrot mixture.
8. Cover the casserole dish and bake for 25 minutes.

ESCALLOPED POTATOES

Probably one of the most fattening recipes in the book, which is why you want to share it with family and friends . . . that way you won't feel as guilty eating it!

SERVES: 8   PREPARATION TIME: 15–20 MINUTES
COOKING TIME: 1½ HOURS

3 tablespoons butter or margarine, softened
4 medium Idaho Russet potatoes, peeled and sliced 1/8 inch thick
½ cup grated Gruyère cheese
½ cup grated Parmesan cheese
1 cup heavy cream
1 teaspoon salt
½ teaspoon pepper

1. Preheat the oven to 350°F.
2. Grease (using butter or cooking spray) a 1½-quart casserole dish.
3. Arrange a layer of potatoes in the baking dish; sprinkle some of both cheeses over them. Continue layering potatoes and cheeses, ending with a layer of potatoes.
4. In a bowl, whisk together the cream, salt, and pepper and pour over the potatoes.
5. Dot the top with butter and bake for 1 to 1½ hours or until the potatoes are tender and golden brown.
6. Cool for 5 minutes before serving.

CRANBERRY LACE COOKiES

A delicious semi-healthy cookie. After all, it has oats, dried cranberries, and nuts—
how bad can it be?

MAKES: 6 DOZEN   PREPARATION TIME: 20 MINUTES
COOKING TIME: 8 MINUTES PER BATCH

⅔ cup flour
½ teaspoon salt
½ teaspoon baking soda
½ cup rolled oats (old-fashionoed oats)
1½ sticks butter or margarine
⅔ cup brown sugar
⅔ cup white sugar
1 extra-large egg, lightly beaten
1 teaspoon vanilla
2 cups chopped pecans
⅔ cup dried cranberries (Craisins)

1. Preheat the oven to 350°F. Line a baking sheet with baker's parchment.
2. Blend in a bowl the flour, salt, baking soda, and rolled oats
3. In a mixer cream together the butter, sugars, egg, and vanilla.
4. Add the dry mixture to the creamed mixture and combine thoroughly. Add the pecans and cranberries.
5. Drop the batter by the teaspoon onto the parchment.
6. Bake each tray of cookies for 8 to 10 minutes.
7. Cool the cookies slightly on baking sheet, then remove to a cooling rack.

✳ You can use the same sheet of parchment paper numerous times, as the cookies come right off the paper.

EDITH'S ORANGE CAKE

Edith made this cake a lot (and we mean a lot!) due to overwhelming requests, holiday or not!
It tastes great served with a scoop of vanilla ice cream.

SERVES: 8–10   PREPARATION TIME: 10 MINUTES
COOKING TIME: 50–60 MINUTES

CAKE

1 18.25-ounce package orange cake mix
1 3.4-ounce package instant vanilla pudding
½ cup vegetable oil
1 cup orange juice
4 extra-large eggs

1. Preheat the oven to 350°F.
2. Grease a 10-inch Bundt pan using oil, cooking spray, or Baker's Joy. (I prefer Baker's Joy for baking.)
3. Mix all of the ingredients together and beat for 2 minutes.
4. Pour the batter into the Bundt pan and bake for 50 to 60 minutes. The cake is done when it is golden and bounces back when touched.
5. When the cake is completely cool, remove it from the pan.

ORANGE GLAZE

2 cups confectioner's sugar
3½ tablespoons orange juice

Mix the confectioners' sugar with the orange juice, and pour the glaze over the cooled cake.

✳ You can substitute milk for the orange juice to make an unflavored glaze.

DEDE'S SOUR CREAM COFFEE CAKE

A family friend makes this every year for Rosh Hashanah. It's moist and great for either dessert or breakfast with coffee or tea.

SERVES: 8–10   PREPARATION TIME: 25 MINUTES
COOKING TIME: 40–45 MINUTES

TOPPING AND FILLING
⅓ cup brown sugar (light or dark)
¼ cup white sugar
1 teaspoon cinnamon
¼ cup finely chopped pecans

CAKE
½ cup butter
1 cup sugar
2 eggs
2 cups presifted all-purpose flour
1 teaspoon baking soda
1 teaspoon baking powder
½ teaspoon salt
1 cup sour cream
1 teaspoon vanilla

1. In a small bowl, combine the sugars, cinnamon, and pecans for the topping and filling. Set aside.
2. Coat a 10-inch Bundt pan with cooking spray.
3. Preheat the oven to 325°F.
4. For the cake, cream the butter until soft, then add the sugar and cream the mixture well until light and fluffy.

5. Add the eggs one at a time, beating well after each one.
6. Mix together the flour, baking soda, baking powder, and salt.
7. Add the dry ingredients to the creamed mixture gradually, alternating with the sour cream.
8. Add the vanilla, and mix well.
9. Pour half of the cake batter into the Bundt pan and then cover with half of the topping and filling mixture.
10. Pour the remaining batter over the filling mixture, and then top that batter with the remainder of the filling mixture.
11. Bake for 40 to 45 minutes. The cake is done when the outside is golden and bounces back when touched lightly.
12. Let the cake cool on a rack, then remove it from the pan.

KATIE'S LEMON CAKE

This recipe has been in the Marks repertoire since Roz's bridal shower.

SERVES: 8–10   PREPARATION TIME: 15 MINUTES
COOKING TIME: 40–60 MINUTES

CAKE

1 18.25 oz box yellow cake mix
1 3-ounce package lemon Jell-O
¾ cup vegetable oil
¾ cup water
1 teaspoon lemon extract
4 extra-large eggs

1. Preheat the oven to 350°F.
2. In a stand mixer, combine the cake mix and Jell-O mix. Add the oil, water, and lemon extract, and blend well.
3. Add the eggs one at a time.
4. Grease and flour a 10-inch tube or Bundt pan, using cooking spray or Baker's Joy.
5. Pour the batter into the pan.
6. Bake for 40 to 60 minutes. The cake is done when it is golden.
7. Cool the cake for 15 to 20 minutes before removing it from the pan.

iCiNG

2 tablespoons butter
3 tablespoons milk
1 teaspoon lemon zest
3 tablespoons lemon juice
2 cups confectioners' sugar

1. Heat the butter and milk until the butter melts.
2. Add the lemon zest, lemon juice, and confectioners' sugar. Stir well.
3. Pour the icing over the cooled cake.

BLONDE BROWNiES

A foolproof recipe, these brownies are "blonde" as opposed to the usual all-chocolate fudge brownies. Though not traditionally Jewish, they disappear as quickly as you set them out!

SERVES: 10–12   PREPARATION TIME: 20–25 MINUTES
COOKING TIME: 20–25 MINUTES

⅓ cup unsalted butter, melted
1 cup light brown sugar
1 extra-large egg, beaten
1 teaspoon vanilla
1 cup presifted all-purpose flour
½ teaspoon baking powder
⅛ teaspoon baking soda
⅛ teaspoon salt
6 ounces semisweet chocolate chips

1. Preheat the oven to 350°F.
2. Melt the butter in a saucepan, then remove from the heat and add the sugar.
3. Pour the mixture into a medium-sized mixing bowl.
4. Add the beaten egg and the vanilla.
5. Mix together the flour, baking powder, baking soda, and salt, then add to the butter mixture a little at a time.
6. Add the chocolate chips. Mix well.
7. Spread the batter in a 9 x 13-inch baking pan greased with baking spray.
8. Bake for 20 to 25 minutes.

* This amount of chocolate chips works well, but for those who like less chocolate, try 3 ounces instead.

CHOCOLATE CHiP BANANA BREAD

One of the most requested desserts in Roz's recipe bin (aside from the Mandelbrot),
this banana bread is, quite simply, amazing.

SERVES: 8–10   PREPARATION TIME: 30 MINUTES
COOKING TIME: 90 MINUTES

½ cup butter or margarine, softened
1⅔ cups sugar
2 extra-large eggs, lightly beaten
1½ teaspoons baking powder
½ teaspoon baking soda
4 tablespoons sour cream
2 cups flour
½ teaspoon salt
1 cup mashed banana (approximately 4 bananas)
1 teaspoon vanilla
2 cups mini chocolate chips (12-ounce bag)

1. Preheat the oven to 350°F.
2. Cream the butter and sugar, then add the eggs and beat well.
3. Dissolve the baking powder and soda in the sour cream, then add to the butter mixture.
4. Gradually add the flour and salt. Mix well.
5. Add the mashed bananas. Mix well.
6. Add the vanilla and finally the chocolate chips.
7. Grease a 5 x 9-inch loaf pan (or two smaller loaf pans) with baking spray.
8. Scrape the batter into the pan(s).
9. Bake the bread(s) for approximately 90 minutes or until lightly browned and firm.
10. Cool and remove the bread(s) from the pan(s).

✳ These breads freeze well.

MATZO BRICKLE FOR PASSOVER

A friend of ours brought this dessert to a seder Roz hosted years ago, and it was so good we begged her for the recipe. Thanks, Arlene!

SERVES: 10–12   PREPARATION TIME: 20 MINUTES
COOKING TIME: 4–5 MINUTES

4 sheets matzo
1 cup (2 sticks) butter or margarine
1 cup packed dark brown sugar
12 ounces (2 cups) chocolate chips
1 cup coarsely ground walnuts or almonds

1. Preheat oven to 450°F.
2. Line a large cookie sheet with sides (or a jellyroll pan) with heavy-duty aluminum foil.
3. Lay out the matzo as close as possible in one layer in pan, breaking the pieces to fit.
4. Melt the butter with brown sugar in a saucepan, stirring frequently until it bubbles.
5. Pour the mixture over the matzo and spread to coat.
6. Put the pan in the oven for 1 to 2 minutes, and then remove.
7. Sprinkle the chocolate chips over the top and return the pan to the oven for another 1 to 2 minutes or until the chocolate softens.
8. Remove the pan from the oven and, using a spatula, spread the chocolate to cover the matzo.
9. Sprinkle the nuts over the chocolate.
10. Place the pan in the freezer for 20 minutes or until hard.
11. Remove and "crack" up matzo, remove the foil from bottom, and put the brickle in a plastic container or ziplock bags.
12. Store in the refrigerator or freezer until ready to serve.

PASSOVER TART

This is another of Arlene's Passover desserts that we all love. Passover is a long holiday, and you can never have too many good desserts to get you through the week.

SERVES: 8–10 PREPARATION TIME: 15–20 MINUTES
COOKING TIME: 12–15 MINUTES

2¼ cups ground nuts (walnuts or pecans)
3 tablespoons butter or margarine, melted
⅓ cup sugar
1 12-ounce bag semisweet chocolate chips
1–2 pints raspberries or strawberries

1. Preheat the oven to 350°F.
2. Mix together the nuts, butter, and sugar to make the crust.
3. Press the mixture into the bottom and sides of a 9-inch glass pie plate.
4. Bake the crust for 12 to 15 minutes or until browned.
5. Remove from the oven and cool.
6. Melt the chocolate in a pan and brush two-thirds of the chocolate onto the bottom and sides of the cooled crust.
7. Arrange the berries on the chocolate before the chocolate hardens.
8. Drizzle the remaining third of the melted chocolate over the berries.
9. Refrigerate until ready to serve.

APPLE CRiSP

This is a recipe where you can substitute peaches or blueberries for the apples. Rather than buying canned fruit or fruit filling, I always use fresh fruit. This easy dessert can be made ahead of time and then reheated in the oven.

SERVES: 6   PREPARATION TIME: 20 MINUTES
COOKING TIME: 40–45 MINUTES

4 cups peeled and sliced tart apples (Granny Smiths are great!)
2 tablespoons sugar
½ teaspoon cinnamon, divided
¼ cup orange juice
2 cup presifted all-purpose flour
⅛ teaspoon salt
¼ teaspoon nutmeg (optional)
⅓ cup brown sugar
3 tablespoons margarine or butter, melted

1. Preheat the oven to 350°F.
2. Peel and slice the apples into a large bowl.
3. Combine the sugar and ¼ teaspoon cinnamon, sprinkle over the sliced apples, and toss to coat them.
4. Grease with cooking spray or butter a 1½–2-quart casserole dish or an 8 x 8-inch glass baking dish.
5. Spread the apples in the baking dish and sprinkle with the orange juice.
6. Combine the flour, salt, ¼ teaspoon cinnamon, nutmeg, and brown sugar.
7. Add the melted butter to the dry ingredients and stir to make a "crumbly" topping.
8. Spread the topping over the apples.
9. Bake uncovered for 40 to 45 minutes or until lightly browned and the apples are tender.

✳ Serve with vanilla ice cream or whipped cream, or both!

COMFORT FOODS

Two Chinese men are coming out of a Jewish restaurant, and one says to the other:
"The problem with Jewish food is that two days later, you're hungry again."

As Nancy mentioned in her Foreword, it's no secret that for Jewish families food is an expression of love, comfort, and tradition. Who hasn't felt better after a delicious popover, hot soup, or indulgent pot roast? Here we've presented you with some real Jewish classics (kasha and varnishkas) alongside better-known comfort foods like apple strudel and cheesecake. They may not be holiday classics, but they're strong, hearty foods that will warm your body and hopefully your spirits!

ALLAN'S FAVORITE SWISS STEAK

This recipe was given to Roz at her bridal shower thirty-eight years ago by her mother-in-law. At first glance the recipe doesn't look too enticing, but when it is cooked and served with the mashed potatoes, you'll be smacking your lips.

SERVES: 4–6   PREPARATION TIME: 15–20 MINUTES
COOKING TIME: 1½ HOURS

1–2 pounds top-round steak
1 teaspoon vegetable oil
1 clove garlic, minced
2–2½ cups sliced Vidalia onion
1 8-ounce bottle mild chili sauce
¼ cup water

1. Preheat the oven to 325°F.
2. Cut the top-round steak into small cubed pieces and brown in the oil with the garlic.
3. Once browned, place the beef into a casserole dish and place the sliced onion on top.
4. Add the chili sauce diluted with the water.
5. Cover and bake for 1½ hours.
6. Serve with mashed potatoes (see page 158).

JEWISH BBQ BRISKET

Andrea's good friend Ryan is not only a great cook but also a true master of the grill, always feeding his large group of friends (and their wives and kids and dogs). In fact, his lucky wife, Staci, hardly ever has to make dinner! When he told us about his recipe for brisket from the grill, we knew we needed to include it. After trying many recipes and techniques over the years, Ryan combined the best parts of all of them to create his own unique smoky flavor and part-grill/part-oven cooking style. It may not be for the brisket beginner, but if you love good barbecue, it's definitely one to try!

SERVES: 8–10
PREPARATION TIME: 1½ HOURS THE NIGHT BEFORE AND
ABOUT 2 HOURS THE DAY OF
COOKING TIME: ABOUT 7 HOURS

DRY RUB

8 tablespoons light brown sugar

3 tablespoons kosher salt

1 tablespoon chili powder

½ teaspoon black pepper

½ teaspoon cayenne pepper (you can sub more chili powder if you don't like spicy)

½ teaspoon jalapeño seasoning (easy to find in any grocery store)

½ teaspoon Old Bay seasoning

½ teaspoon onion powder

½ teaspoon dry rubbed thyme

BRISKET BBQ

6–8-pound first-cut brisket, trimmed (with only a small layer of fat on top, about ⅛–¼ inch thick)

4–6 garlic cloves

24–64 ounces apple juice

¼ cup olive oil

3 Spanish onions, sliced

1 quart low-sodium beef broth (organic is better)

1 tablespoon kosher salt

Black pepper to taste (about 1 teaspoon)

1 teaspoon onion powder

1 teaspoon garlic powder

1 cup chili sauce

1 cup ketchup

1 cup brown sugar

10–12 medium Yukon gold potatoes, halved

The Night Before

1. Mix the dry rub ingredients together and set aside for about an hour.
2. Using a paring knife, make small cuts in the brisket in random places. Place whole, peeled garlic cloves in the slits.
3. Coat the surface of the meat liberally with the dry rub. Tightly double-wrap the brisket in foil and refrigerate overnight.

The Day Of

1. Preheat the broiler to the maximum temperature.
2. Take the brisket out and let it sit for about an hour, to return to room temperature. In the meantime, begin preparing your smoker or grill.
3. When the brisket has returned to room temperature, place it in a large roasting pan and put it under the broiler for about 5 minutes to brown, then flip it and brown the other side. You can do this on very hot grill as well. You are trying to lock in the juices with a nice char on the outside.
4. Once you are done searing the meat on both sides, place the brisket in your smoker, fat-side up, and smoke the brisket for about 3 to 4 hours depending on how hot your smoker gets. If you are using a gas grill as a smoker, you will need to go with the 4 hours; just keep an eye on your temperature.

5. Baste the brisket with apple juice (or use a squirt bottle) every 30 minutes or so.

6. While the brisket is smoking, heat a skillet to medium and drizzle with the oil. Place the sliced onions in the skillet and caramelize them for about 20 to 30 minutes, then set them aside. Mix together the remaining ingredients, except for the potatoes, and set the liquid aside.

7. Preheat the oven to 350°F.

8. Once the brisket has finished smoking, place it in a roasting pan and cover it with the onions and the liquid mixture (or as much of the liquid as will fit in the pan without making it too full). Place the potatoes along the side of the roasting pan. Cover the pan and cook for about 2½ to 3 hours or until the potatoes are tender and the meat is almost falling apart.

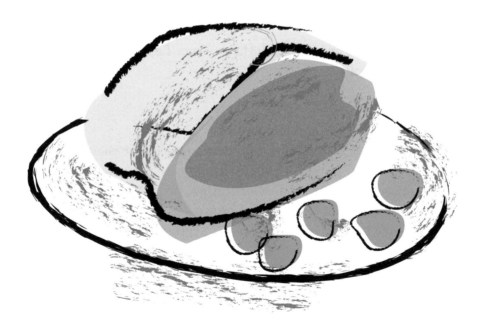

9. Remove the brisket from the liquid and let it rest for about 1 hour. Remove the potatoes and set them aside.
10. Pour the remaining liquid and onions into a pot. Bring to a simmer and reduce by one-third, to serve as a gravy.
11. When the brisket has cooled, slice against the grain about ¼ inch thick and return the slices to the roasting pan. Pour some of the gravy on top, surround the meat with potatoes, and reheat in the oven at low temperature.
12. Serve when ready with gravy on the side.

✳ You can do all of this a day in advance, and everything will be just as good.

✳ Ryan tells us that he's used his gas grill as a smoker, and it has worked well. You are not looking for an overwhelming smoky flavor, just a hint. There are plenty of Web sites and books that will teach you how to use your gas grill as a smoker.

✳ Use any wood chips you like. Ryan personally likes fruit tree wood chips, apple or cherry or a combination of both, because they are not very intense with their smoke taste.

MASHED POTATOES

I don't know anyone who doesn't love mashed potatoes. We add a little onion and cheddar cheese just to spiffy it up a little. Feel free to leave out the minced onion and cheese, but you will truly be missing something delicious.

SERVES: 6–8   PREPARATION TIME: 15 MINUTES
COOKING TIME: 20–25 MINUTES

6 medium Idaho Russet potatoes, peeled and cut into chunks
¼ pound (1 stick) butter
½ cup milk
¼ cup sour cream
2 tablespoons dehydrated minced onions (optional)
¾ teaspoon salt (to taste)
Pepper (to taste)
8 ounces shredded cheddar cheese (optional)

1. Put the potatoes in a pot and cover with cold water. Bring the water to a boil, cover the pot, and simmer for 20 to 25 minutes.
2. When the potatoes are tender, drain and mash them. Add the butter, milk, sour cream, minced onion (optional), salt, and pepper. Mix well.
3. Stir in the grated cheddar cheese (optional) and put the pot over low heat for approximately 3–4 minutes to melt the cheese.

STUFFED TOMATOES

Roz was always looking for ways to get the family to eat tomatoes. Adding onion, garlic, bread crumbs, and cheese worked! This side dish goes with any meal and is impressive enough to serve to company as well.

SERVES: 6   PREPARATION TIME: 20 MINUTES
COOKING TIME: 20–25 MINUTES

6 medium tomatoes
2 tablespoons olive oil
3 tablespoons chopped Vidalia onion (or shallots)
1–2 cloves garlic, mashed
¼ cup bread crumbs
¾ cup shredded mozzarella cheese, divided
¼ teaspoon salt
⅛ teaspoon pepper

1. Cut the top quarter off the tomatoes, then cut a very thin sliver off of the bottoms so they will sit upright. Using your knife, clean out the insides of the tomatoes as best you can without tearing the outer skin. Discard the seeds, but keep and coarsely chop the tomato flesh.
2. In a saucepan heat the olive oil and sauté the onions and garlic.
3. Add the reserved chopped tomato and sauté for 5 to 6 minutes or until everything is soft.
4. Remove from the heat and add the bread crumbs, ½ cup of the mozzarella cheese, and salt and pepper.
5. Preheat the oven to 350°F. Coat a shallow baking dish with cooking spray.
6. Spoon the stuffing mixture into the hollowed tomatoes and place them in the baking dish.
7. Sprinkle the tops with the remaining ¼ cup mozzarella cheese. You can refrigerate the stuffed tomatoes at this point, if making the dish ahead.
8. Bring the tomatoes to room temperature (if refrigerated) and bake for 20 to 25 minutes or until the cheese on top is melted.

SAUTÉED BROCCOLI OR CAULIFLOWER

This recipe came about as a way to use leftover broccoli and cauliflower. It seems there is always steamed broccoli or cauliflower left at the end of the night! We now make this instead of steamed broccoli or cauliflower, although it isn't quite as low-calorie.

SERVES: 4–6   PREPARATION TIME: 10–15 MINUTES
COOKING TIME: 30 MINUTES

1 12-ounce package each fresh broccoli florets or cauliflower, or 1 fresh head of
    broccoli or cauliflower
2 tablespoons margarine
1 small Vidalia onion
1 tablespoon lemon, or to your taste
Salt and pepper to taste

1. Steam the broccoli or cauliflower for a few minutes (you want it crisp not mushy), and drain in a colander.
2. Melt the margarine and sauté the onion for about 3 to 4 minutes.
3. Add the broccoli or cauliflower and continue to sauté for 10 to 15 minutes, until the veggies start to brown.
4. Add the lemon, salt, and pepper to taste.

✱ You can make the recipe using both the broccoli and cauliflower together.

POT ROAST

You can include potatoes with the roast, or serve it with Potato Varenikas (similar to pierogis—see below) along with French green beans.

SERVES: 8   PREPARATION TIME: 20–25 MINUTES
COOKING TIME: 3½ HOURS

1 tablespoon vegetable oil
2½–3-pound boneless chuck roast (or a 3-pound brisket)
2 garlic cloves, minced
2 small onions, cut in chunks
1 10-ounce can beef broth
2 tomatoes, cut in chunks
1 bay leaf
¾ cup red wine
1 teaspoon salt
½ teaspoon pepper
4 carrots
3 potatoes, peeled and cut in chunks (optional)

1. Heat the oil in a Dutch oven and brown the beef.
2. Add the garlic and onions, and sauté until the onions are golden.
3. Add the beef broth, tomatoes, bay leaf, red wine, salt, and pepper. Bring to a boil, then turn down to a low simmer and cover the pot.
4. Gently simmer on top of the stove for 2½ hours. Then add the carrots and potatoes (optional) and simmer for 1 more hour.

✳ You can cook the roast in the oven as well. Follow the instructions above until you bring the broth and wine to a boil, then place the covered pot in a preheated 325°F oven for 2½ hours. Then add the carrots and cook for 1 more hour.

POTATO VARENIKAS

Roz grew up watching and helping her Aunt Frieda and her grandmother make these little potato dumplings (also called pierogis) on the kitchen table—rolling the dough and mashing the potatoes, filling the cut dough with the potatoes, and then pinching the dough closed so that the potatoes wouldn't spill out during boiling. This is a recipe you can do with your children, and it will create memories.

SERVES: 8 (MAKES 20–25)   PREPARATION TIME: 60 MINUTES
COOKING TIME: 5 MINUTES

DOUGH
5 cups presifted all-purpose flour
2 teaspoons salt
4 large eggs
1 cup low-fat milk
¾ cup water

1. Combine the flour and salt.
2. In a separate bowl, mix the eggs, milk, and water.
3. Add the liquid to the flour and salt, and mix to form a dough. The dough should be soft enough that it sticks to the bottom of the bowl, but still holds its shape. (You can always add more liquid or flour to get the right consistency.)
4. Cover and let the dough sit at room temperature for 1 hour.

POTATO FiLLiNG
3 cups potatoes, peeled and cut in chunks (about 3–4 medium potatoes)
⅓ cup margarine
¼ cup grated onion
1 teaspoon salt
½ teaspoon pepper
4 tablespoons melted margarine

1. Place the potatoes in a pot of cold water and bring to a boil. Partially cover the pot and simmer until the potatoes are tender.
2. Drain and mash the potatoes, adding ⅓ cup margarine, grated onion, and salt and pepper to taste.
3. Lightly flour a flat surface, and divide the dough in half.
4. Working with half the dough at a time, roll it out as thin as possible without tearing it.
5. Using a 3-inch can, drinking glass, or cookie or biscuit cutter, cut rounds out of the dough.
6. Place 1 tablespoon of the potato filling in the center of the round of dough, fold over the top half, and pinch the edges closed.
7. Repeat with the remaining dough, reforming and recutting to use up all the scraps. There should be enough filling and dough to make about 20 to 25 pierogis.
8. Bring a large pot of salted water to a boil, and drop about half of the pierogis at a time into the pot. They are cooked when they rise to the top and float, about 5 to 10 minutes.
9. Remove them with a slotted spoon and put in a saucepan with melted margarine. Bring them up to heat and serve.

✳ You can always use an electric hand beater rather than a masher for the potatoes.

MIMI CHICKEN

Our good friend Mimi gave us the recipe for this dish years ago, and it ended up being one of our favorites of all time. In fact, it came with no name and is now known across many Miami households as "Mimi Chicken." Though not traditionally Jewish, we just couldn't leave it out. It's a great dinner recipe when you're expecting a crowd (serve it family style), and the leftovers are just as good!

SERVES: 4–6   PREPARATION TIME: 20–25 MINUTES
COOKING TIME: 1½–2 HOURS

1 teaspoon olive oil
1 clove garlic, minced
1 small onion, cut in thin slices
Salt and pepper
1 whole chicken cut up, or 3 breasts (bone-in) cut in half plus 6 wings cut in half
1 cup low-sodium beef broth
3 tablespoons tomato paste
1 cup white wine (sweet vermouth or any white cooking wine)
¾ cup pitted green olives
2 packages Sazon seasoning (a Spanish seasoning, it can be found in all grocery stores in the spice aisle)

1. Put the olive oil, garlic, and onion in a 10-inch frying pan with lid and start sautéing.
2. Lightly salt and pepper the chicken pieces and add them to the pan to brown.
3. When the chicken is browned (about 15 minutes), add the beef broth and bring to a simmer.

4. Add the tomato paste, white wine, and olives, and continue simmering over low heat for about 1 hour, partially covering the pan. Stir occasionally, and add more beef broth or wine if necessary.
5. After an hour, add the Sazon seasoning.
6. The chicken is done when the meat is tender and almost falls off the bone.
7. Serve with Kasha Varnishkas (or yellow or saffron rice).

* You can also add vegetables to the pot to make it even more delicious. We like carrots and string beans.

* You can also make the recipe with just wings, using at least 14 wings cut in half.

WINE SUGGESTIONS

White: Villa Mt. Eden Grand Reserve Chardonnay (California)

Red: Alamos Malbec (Argentina)

STUFFED CABBAGE

We tried out this true Jewish classic recipe on Andrea's non-Jewish husband and one picky fifteen-month-old. The verdict? An empty plate. Don't let the ingredients scare you . . . it's truly delicious.

SERVES: 6–8   PREPARATION TIME: 45–60 MINUTES
COOKING TIME: 3 HOURS

1 2–3-pound head of green cabbage
1 can (28-ounce) crushed tomatoes
1 can (8-ounce) tomato sauce
½ teaspoon salt
¼ teaspoon pepper
½ cup ketchup
½ cup brown sugar (light or dark)
4–5 tablespoons lemon juice
½ cup raisins
1 pound ground sirloin
3 tablespoons uncooked white rice
4 tablespoons grated onion
1 egg
3 tablespoons cold water

1. In a large pot with a lid, pour boiling water over the head of cabbage, cover, and let sit 20 minutes. This softens the cabbage leaves and makes it easier to remove them one at a time
2. While cabbage is softening, make the sauce and the meat mixture.
3. For the sauce, in a large bowl combine the crushed tomatoes, tomato sauce, salt, pepper, ketchup, brown sugar, lemon juice, and raisins. Mix well.

166

4. In a separate bowl, combine the ground beef, rice, grated onion, egg, and water. Mix well.
5. Preheat the oven to 325°F.
6. After the cabbage has softened, remove it from the pot of water and start removing the leaves carefully. You'll probably need between 10 and 12 leaves.
7. Trim off the hard portion at the base of each leaf.
8. For each cabbage roll, place 1 tablespoon meat filling near the base of the leaf and roll it up, tucking in the sides like an envelope. If you run out of large leaves, you can overlap 2 small leaves together.
9. Place the stuffed cabbage rolls in a large casserole, seam-side down. Do the same with the second layer if necessary.
10. Pour the sauce over the cabbage rolls, cover tightly, and bake for 3 hours.

WINE SUGGESTIONS

Red: Cape Indaba Pinotage (South Africa)

White: Saint M. Riesling (Germany)

CABBAGE BORSCHT

Cabbage Borscht is definitely a love-it-or-hate-it dish. We love it. And for those who think like us, we're happy to share!

SERVES: 8–10   PREPARATION TIME: 30 MINUTES
COOKING TIME: 4½ HOURS

2 pounds flanken, cut into large chunks
3–3½-pound head of green cabbage
3 quarts water
1 28-ounce can chopped tomatoes
Juice of 1 lemon (approximately ⅛ cup)
1¼–1½ cups light brown sugar
1½–2 teaspoons sour salt

1. Spray an 8-quart lidded pot with cooking spray and brown the flanken on all sides.
2. Cut the cabbage into small to medium-sized pieces and put it into the pot over the browned flanken.
3. Pour 3 quarts of water over the cabbage and meat; then add the chopped tomatoes, lemon, brown sugar, and sour salt. Bring everything to a boil, then lower the heat to a simmer.
4. Simmer the soup partially covered for 3 hours, checking and stirring every hour.
5. After 3 hours, taste the soup and if necessary add more brown sugar, sour salt, and lemon to taste.
6. Simmer partially covered for another 1½ hours. The longer it cooks, the better it gets.
7. Serve the cabbage soup and flanken in big bowls with pumpernickel bread on the side.

✳ The soup is done when the beef is falling off the bones.

DOTTiE'S NOODLE PUDDiNG

Yes, another noodle pudding recipe! You can never have enough of them—they are all different and equally delicious. This one has a crunchy crust that forms on the top. Roz's neighbor used to make this for the holidays when she was growing up and gave Roz the recipe many years ago.

SERVES: 6–8   PREPARATION TIME: 20 MINUTES
COOKING TIME: 60 MINUTES

1 8-ounce package medium egg noodles
4 tablespoons butter or margarine, softened
3 ounces cream cheese
¼ cup sugar
3 eggs
1 cup orange juice
4½ cup crushed cornflakes
¾ stick butter or margarine, softened
⅓ cup sugar
1½ tablespoons cinnamon

1. Preheat the oven to 350°F.
2. Cook the noodles according to the directions on the package and drain.
3. In a large bowl mix the noodles with the butter so that the butter melts.
4. Pour the noodle mixture into a 9 x 13-inch glass baking dish well greased with cooking spray.
5. In a blender, mix well the cream cheese, sugar, eggs, and orange juice.
6. Pour the mixture over the noodles.
7. For the topping mix the remaining ingredients together, and sprinkle them over the noodle mixture.
8. Bake the pudding for 1 hour or until golden.

CINNAMON APPLE STRUDEL

There is always room for fruit desserts, especially apple strudel. It's not that hard and looks quite impressive. Tastes better than any strudel you could ever buy at a bakery.

SERVES: 8–10   PREPARATION TIME: 20 –30 MINUTES
COOKING TIME: 30–35 MINUTES

3 apples (Gala or Granny Smiths), peeled, cored, thinly sliced and cut into ¼-inch
  pieces
½ cup raisins (golden raisins look prettier but aren't necessary)
½ cup brown sugar, firmly packed
½ teaspoon lemon juice
1 teaspoon cinnamon
2 tablespoons sweet unsalted butter, diced
6 sheets phyllo dough (keep wrapped in the refrigerator until ready to use)
1 stick sweet unsalted butter, melted
4 tablespoons cinnamon sugar (4 tablespoons white sugar mixed with 1 teaspoon
  cinnamon)

1. Preheat the oven to 350°F.
2. Line a baking sheet with baker's parchment.
3. In a bowl, combine the apples, raisins, brown sugar, lemon juice, cinnamon, and diced butter. Mix well.
4. Remove the cold phyllo dough from the box. (Keeping it cold makes it easy to work with.)
5. Place 1 sheet of phyllo pastry on the parchment and brush with the melted butter. Do the same with 5 more sheets, stacking them on top of each other one at a time and brushing them with the melted butter.

6. Spoon the apple mixture down the left (long) side of the phyllo rectangle, leaving a 2-inch border on the top, bottom, and the side where the filling is.

7. Fold the top edge down and the bottom edge up to cover the filling (like an egg roll).

8. Gently roll the stack of pastry up along the long side to enclose the filling.

9. Brush the strudel with melted butter and sprinkle heavily with the cinnamon sugar.

10. Bake for 30 to 35 minutes or until golden.

11. Let the strudel cool, then remove carefully and place on a serving dish.

12. If made ahead of time, wrap the strudel in waxed paper and aluminum foil, then refrigerate or freeze. Reheat the strudel in the oven prior to serving.

✳ Depending on the size of the apples you use, you may have enough apple mixture to make two strudels. If so, you can assemble them both (one at time) on the same baking sheet. Be sure to place the first stack of phyllo near one side of the parchment so you can fit both strudels on the same baking sheet.

✳ Don't worry if the phyllo sheets tear—with 6 pieces, you can overlap the torn parts, and no one will ever know the difference!

✳ If you don't have a pastry brush to brush the melted butter onto the phyllo dough, you can spread it using the back of a tablespoon.

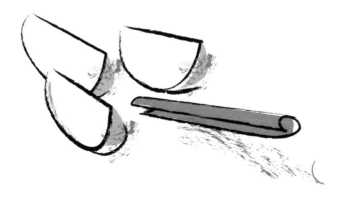

DELICIOUS CLASSIC CHEESECAKE WITH AN OREO COOKIE CRUST

Andrea's brother David is a picky eater. He's one of those people who have "rules" about what foods he will and will not eat and is famous for his nonsensical critiques of any and all menu selections. This cheesecake is his very favorite dessert. The first time he tried it, it actually inspired several phone calls from him to both Andrea and her husband, expressing his sincere sorrow that they were not there to taste it and imploring them to drive over to Roz's house immediately to sample a piece. Seriously.

SERVES: 8–10   PREPARATION TIME: 20 MINUTES
COOKING TIME: 65–75 MINUTES

24 Oreo cookies
1 cup chopped pecans
6 tablespoons margarine or butter, melted
3 8-ounce packages cream cheese
¾ cup sugar
1 tablespoon vanilla
3 extra-large eggs
¼ cup caramel topping
¼ cup chocolate chips
4 teaspoons skim or regular milk

1. Preheat the oven to 300°F.
2. To make the crust, pulse the Oreo cookies and pecans in a food processor until they become crumbs, then add the melted butter and pulse quickly to mix them well.
3. Spray a 9- or 10-inch springform pan with cooking spray and then press the cookie mixture into the bottom and about 1½ to 2 inches up the sides of the springform pan. (Don't worry if the sides of the crust are not even all around; the cheesecake is so delicious no one will even notice.)

4. Refrigerate the crust for 10 minutes.
5. For the filling, using a stand mixer beat the cream cheese, sugar, and vanilla on medium speed until well blended.
6. Add the eggs one at a time, blending well.
7. Pour the filling into the Oreo crust.
8. Bake the cheesecake for 65 to 75 minutes or until the center is set.
9. Cool completely before removing the sides of the springform pan.
10. Drizzle the caramel sauce over the cooled cheesecake.
11. Melt the chocolate chips with the milk over the stove or microwave until melted and drizzle this sauce over the cheesecake as well.
12. Refrigerate for at least 5 hours before serving.

* As a variation on caramel and chocolate, you can top the cheesecake with fresh strawberries or blueberries instead.

BANANA CAKE

This is an alternative to banana bread. It is very light and airy, like cake. You can make it in a 9 x 13-inch baking dish, or you can make it in a loaf pan like a banana bread.

SERVES: 8–10   PREPARATION TIME: 15–20 MINUTES
COOKING TIME: 50–60 MINUTES

7 extra-large eggs
2 cups sugar
2¼ cups flour
1 teaspoon baking soda
1 teaspoon baking powder
4 ripe bananas
½ cup vegetable oil
1 teaspoon vanilla

1. Preheat the oven to 350°F.
2. Break the eggs into two bowls, separating the whites and yolks.
3. Beat the egg whites until they form soft peaks.
4. Beat the sugar into the egg whites, little by little. Then beat in the egg yolks, one by one.
5. Mix the flour with the baking soda and baking powder.
6. Add the flour mixture to the egg-and-sugar mixture.
7. Beat in the bananas, oil, and vanilla.
8. Pour the batter into a greased 9 x 13-inch baking pan or into 2 loaf pans (5 x 9 inches).
9. Bake the cake(s) for 50 to 60 minutes or until golden brown.

GRANDMA ROSE'S POPOVER RECIPE
(Courtesy of Nancy Ratzan)

In 2003, Nancy traveled to China as part of a delegation of nine religious leaders investigating the role the United Nations plays in Chinese family planning. During this incredible journey, a few of the delegates were sent to a small, rural township in the Gansu province of China, where the average annual family income is $300. As they conducted a random interview, they were invited into the home of a very poor, three-generation family. With great pride and hospitality, the family invited the group to stay for lunch. Though they politely declined, they did stay to taste a freshly baked item. With the first bite, Nancy turned to her translator and said, "Please tell the grandmother that this tastes just like something my Jewish Russian-Polish grandmother used to make for me." The Chinese grandmother asked for her recipe. Nancy told her, and the woman proclaimed (in Chinese), "Yes, yes, that's it. That's how we make it." Food is a powerful connection.

SERVES: 8   PREPARATION TIME: 25 MINUTES
COOKING TIME: 50 MINUTES

3 extra-large eggs
1 cup sifted flour
1 cup milk
3 tablespoons butter, melted
½ teaspoon salt

1. Preheat the oven to 400°F.
2. Beat the eggs in a mixing bowl.
3. Add the flour, milk, butter, and salt. Whisk by hand until blended (but do not overbeat).
4. Pour into eight 5-ounce greased muffin tins.
5. Bake for 40 minutes at 400° or for 50 minutes at 375°.
6. Serve the popovers warm, with strawberry preserves.

RUM POUND CAKE

This is a great go-to recipe that can be made ahead of time. It is delicious served with a little whipped cream and fresh fruit.

SERVES: 8–10   PREPARATION: 20 –25 MINUTES
COOKING TIME: 1½ HOURS

1 cup sweet unsalted butter, softened
1¾ cups sugar
½ teaspoon mace
¼ teaspoon salt
1 teaspoon vanilla
1 jigger (1 tablespoon) rum
5 extra-large eggs
2 cups presifted all-purpose flour

1. Preheat the oven to 300°F.
2. Mix the butter until creamy and gradually blend in the sugar.
3. Add the mace, salt, and vanilla.
4. Beat in 4 eggs, one at a time.
5. Stir in the flour,
6. Beat in the remaining egg.
7. Add the rum and mix well.
8. Spray a 10-inch loaf pan with Baker's Joy or cooking spray and pour in the cake batter.
9. Bake at 300° for 1 hour.
10. Turn the oven down to 250°F and bake for another 30 minutes until the cake is golden and firm. Serve when cool.

* The cake also freezes well. Always wrap in waxed paper and then foil when freezing food. The waxed paper keeps the food from sticking to the foil.

COCONUT PiE

This delicious coconut pie tastes like it took hours to make, yet is very easy. The batter is mixed in a blender and makes its own crust while baking. You can serve the pie warm or cold.

SERVES: 6–8   PREPARATION TIME: 15 MINUTES
COOKING TIME: 40–45 MINUTES

2 cups low-fat milk

¾ cup sugar

½ cup biscuit mix (Bisquick)

4 extra-large eggs

¼ cup butter or margarine, melted

1½ teaspoons vanilla

1 cup coconut

1. Preheat the oven to 350°F.
2. Combine the milk, sugar, biscuit mix, eggs, butter, and vanilla in an electric blender.
3. Cover and blend on low speed for 3 minutes.
4. Grease an 8- to 10-inch pie plate with cooking spray and pour the mixture into it.
5. Let the batter stand for 5 minutes, then sprinkle the coconut on top.
6. Bake the pie for 40 to 45 minutes.

SUPER-RiCH FUDGE CAKE

We have no idea where this recipe came from—we don't recognize the handwriting, and there is no name on it. The best we can assume is that Roz had it at someone's home, loved it, and asked for the recipe. The lesson? Share recipes . . . most people are flattered when you ask.

SERVES: 8–10   PREPARATION TIME: 20–25 MINUTES
COOKING TIME: 50–55 MINUTES

12 ouncees semisweet chocolate chips
1 tablespoon instant coffee mix
5 tablespoons water
1½ cups sweet unsalted butter, softened
2 cups sugar
6 eggs
1 cup flour

1. Preheat the oven to 350°F.
2. Put the chocolate chips, coffee, and water in a double boiler (or a small pot nested in a slightly larger one filled with boiling water).
3. Bring the water in the bottom pot to a boil and keep stirring the chocolate mixture until it melts and the mixture is smooth. Pour the mixture into a bowl to cool.
4. In a large bowl, combine the butter and sugar and beat until creamy.
5. Separate the egg whites and yolks one at a time. Put the whites in a separate small bowl and add the yolks to the creamed mixture one at a time, mixing well after each addition.
6. Gradually beat in the flour, a little at a time. Put the mixture aside for a few minutes. Beat the egg whites until soft peaks form.
7. Gradually and gently, using a flexible spatula, fold the egg whites into the cooled chocolate mixture. Then gently fold the chocolate mixture into the butter and flour mixture.
8. Pour the batter into a greased 9-inch springform pan.
9. Bake the cake for 50 to 55 minutes.

10. Cool the cake and then remove it from the pan.

11. Serve with ice cream or whipped cream.

✳ You can buy whipped cream in a can, already made.

✳ The term "fold" just means to gently mix ingredients together with a spatula in an over-under motion, as opposed to mixing it together with a spoon or fork.

SWEET POTATO PUDDING

When we think of sweet potatoes, most of us think of Thanksgiving. Sweet potatoes are very healthy and go great not just with turkey but as a side dish with chicken and beef. You can make this pudding ahead of time, and for some reason it tastes even better the next day.

SERVES: 6–8   PREPARATION TIME: 15 MINUTES
COOKING TIME: 45–50 MINUTES

8–10 sweet potatoes whole or cut in half depending on the size

4 tablespoons unsalted butter

1 apple (grated or shredded)

3 tablespoons brown sugar

1 teaspoon salt

4 tablespoons orange juice or Mogan David berry wine

1. Preheat the oven to 375°F.

2. Boil the sweet potatoes until soft. Cool.

3. Scoop out the potato pulp, discarding the skin, and mash.

4. Add to the potatoes the butter, grated apple, brown sugar, salt, and orange juice or wine.

5. Mix well and pour into a 1½–2-quart casserole dish greased with cooking spray.

6. Bake the pudding for 45 to 50 minutes.

✳ For special (or not-so-special) occasions, throw on some marshmallows and bake as directed.

METRIC CONVERSION TABLES

APPROXIMATE U.S. METRIC EQUIVALENTS

LIQUID INGREDIENTS

U.S. MEASURES	METRIC	U.S. MEASURES	METRIC
¼ TSP.	1.23 ML	2 TBSP.	29.57 ML
½ TSP.	2.36 ML	3 TBSP.	44.36 ML
¾ TSP.	3.70 ML	¼ CUP	59.15 ML
1 TSP.	4.93 ML	½ CUP	118.30 ML
1¼ TSP.	6.16 ML	1 CUP	236.59 ML
1½ TSP.	7.39 ML	2 CUPS OR 1 PT.	473.18 ML
1¾ TSP.	8.63 ML	3 CUPS	709.77 ML
2 TSP.	9.86 ML	4 CUPS OR 1 QT.	946.36 ML
1 TBSP.	14.79 ML	4 QTS. OR 1 GAL.	3.79 L

DRY INGREDIENTS

U.S. MEASURES		METRIC	U.S. MEASURES	METRIC
17⅗ OZ.	1 LIVRE	500 G	2 OZ.	60 (56.6) G
16 OZ.	1 LB.	454 G	1¾ OZ.	50 G
8⅞ OZ.		250 G	1 OZ.	30 (28.3) G
5¼ OZ.		150 G	⅞ OZ.	25 G
4½ OZ.		125 G	¾ OZ.	21 (21.3) G
4 OZ.		115 (113.2) G	½ OZ.	15 (14.2) G
3½ OZ.		100 G	¼ OZ.	7 (7.1) G
3 OZ.		85 (84.9) G	⅛ OZ.	3½ (3.5) G
2⅘ OZ.		80 G	1/16 OZ.	2 (1.8) G

INDEX

A

alcoholic drinks. *See* specialty drinks; wine
Allan's Favorite Garlic Chicken, 22–23
Allan's Favorite Swiss Steak, 154
Almond Macaroons, 120
Ambrosia (5-Cup Fruit Salad), 59
Andi's Sprite-Roasted Lemon-Pepper Chicken, 82–83
Andrea's tips, 5–6
apples
    about: blessings over honey and, 44
    Apple Crisp, 150–51
    Apple-Raisin Noodle Kugel, 137
    Charoset, 104
    Cinnamon Apple Strudel, 170–71
    Easy Homemade Pear-Infused
        Applesauce, 87
Asparagus with Lemon Sauce, 56
Aunt Judy's Sweet Noodle Pudding, 37
Avocado-Tomato Dip, 10

B

Baby David's Chicken Soup with White
    Meatballs (Matzo Balls), 102
Banana Bread, Chocolate Chip, 147
Banana Cake, 174
beef
    about: brisket, 39
    Allan's Favorite Swiss Steak, 154
    Edith's Red Wine Brisket, 38–39
    Fajitas, 13
    Jewish BBQ Brisket, 154–57
    Pot Roast, 161
    Stuffed Flank Steak, 50–51
    Sweet and Tangy Brisket, 80–81
    Vegetable Soup, 34–35
blessings
    daily, 31–32
    kosher food and, 62
    over candles, 28
    over challah, 28
    over fruit, 129
    over Torah, 129
    over wine, 28, 44
    Rosh Hashanah, 44
    Shabbat, 28
Blintz Soufflé, 58
Blonde Brownies, 146
breads and sandwiches
    about: blessing over bread, 44
    Brisket Paninis, 12
    Chocolate Chip Mandelbrot (Mandel Bread), 42–43
    See also matzo
breaking the fast, 57–68
    about: overview of, 57; wine suggestions, 57
    Blintz Soufflé, 58
    Coleslaw, 65
    Cucumber Salad, 68
    5-Cup Fruit Salad (Ambrosia), 59

Homemade Potato Salad, 64
Rugelach, 66–67
Sarah's Challah French Toast Casserole, 61
Tuna Salad with Dill, 60
brisket. *See* beef
broccoli
    Broccoli Soufflé, 109
    Sautéed Broccoli, 160
    Vegetable Basket, 8–9
    Vegetable Soup, 34–35
burns, treating, 7

C

cabbage
    Cabbage Borscht, 168
    Coleslaw, 65
    Stuffed Cabbage, 166–67
    Vegetable Basket, 8–9
Caipirinha, Kosher, 132–33
cakes. *See* desserts
carrots
    Carrot Cake Cupcakes, 90
    Carrot Tzimmis, 138
    Dilled Carrots, 22
    Vegetable Basket, 8–9
    Vegetable Soup, 34–35
cauliflower
    Sautéed Cauliflower, 160
    Vegetable Basket, 8–9
    Vegetable Soup, 34–35
celery
    Vegetable Basket, 8–9
    Vegetable Soup, 34–35

challah
    blessing over, 28
    Challah Stuffing, 12
    fresh, 15, 16
    for Rosh Hashanah, 30
    Sarah's Challah French Toast
        Casserole, 61
Chanukah, 69–94
    about: dreidel (the game), 93; facts about, 72; lighting menorah, 72; overview of, 69; real world traditions, 70–71; songs for, 77–79, 93–94; spellings of, 81; wine suggestions, 69
    Andi's Sprite-Roasted Lemon-Pepper Chicken, 82–83
    Carrot Cake Cupcakes, 90
    Chocolate Chip Lace Cookies, 92
    Cream Cheese Frosting, 91
    Creamy Vinaigrette Dressing, 89
    Easy Homemade Pear-Infused Applesauce, 87
    Flourless Potato Pancakes, 84–85
    Fruit and Cheese Appetizer, 75
    Honeyed Chicken Wings, 76
    Roasted Vegetables, 88
    Sweet and Tangy Brisket, 80–81
    See also specialty drinks
Charoset, 104
cheese
    Cream Cheese Frosting, 91
    Fruit and Cheese Appetizer, 75
    Mozzarella and Tomato Salad, 49
    Spinach Cheese Squares, 19

chicken
about: cleaning, 23
Allan's Favorite Garlic Chicken, 22–23
Andi's Sprite-Roasted Lemon-Pepper
Chicken, 82–83
Baby David's Chicken Soup with White
Meatballs (Matzo Balls), 102
Chicken Noodle Soup, 48
Chicken Stew, 13
Chopped Liver, 100
Fajitas, 13
Honeyed Chicken Wings, 76
Mimi Chicken, 164–65
chocolate
Aunt Frieda's Nut Cake, 118–19
Blonde Brownies, 146
Chocolate Chip Banana Bread, 147
Chocolate Chip Lace Cookies, 92
Chocolate Chip Mandelbrot (Mandel
Bread), 42–43
Chocolate Fudge Icing, 119
Chocolate-Covered Pretzels and
Strawberries, 135–36
Delicious Classic Cheesecake with an Oreo
Cookie Crust, 172–73
Ice Cream Pie, 26–27
Passover Brownies, 117
Super-Rich Fudge Cake, 178–79
Chopped Liver, 100
Cinnamon Apple Strudel, 170–71
cleaning
chickens, 23
kitchen/utensils, 5

Coconut Pie, 177
Coleslaw, 65
comfort foods, 153–79
about, 153; wine suggestions,
165, 167
Allan's Favorite Swiss Steak, 154
Banana Cake, 174
Cabbage Borscht, 168
Cinnamon Apple Strudel, 170–71
Coconut Pie, 177
Delicious Classic Cheesecake with an
Oreo Cookie Crust, 172–73
Dottie's Noodle Pudding, 169
Grandma Rose's Popover Recipe, 175
Jewish BBQ Brisket, 154–57
Mashed Potatoes, 158
Mimi Chicken, 164–65
Pot Roast, 161
Potato Varenikas, 162–63
Rum Pound Cake, 176
Sautéed Broccoli or Cauliflower, 160
Stuffed Cabbage, 166–67
Stuffed Tomatoes, 159
Super-Rich Fudge Cake, 178–79
Sweet Potato Pudding, 179
conversion charts, 3, 180
Crabmeat Appetizer, 47
Cranberry Lace Cookies, 140
Cream Cheese Frosting, 91
Creamy Vinaigrette Dressing, 89
cucumbers
Cucumber Salad, 68
Vegetable Basket, 8–9

D

Dede's Sour Cream Coffee Cake, 142–43
Delicious Classic Cheesecake with an Oreo
    Cookie Crust, 172–73
desserts
    about: fail-safe crowd-pleaser, 6
    Almond Macaroons, 120
    Apple Crisp, 150–51
    Aunt Frieda's Nut Cake, 118–19
    Aunt Judy's Sweet Noodle Pudding, 37
    Banana Cake, 174
    Blintz Soufflé, 58
    Blonde Brownies, 146
    Carrot Cake Cupcakes, 90
    Chocolate Chip Banana Bread, 147
    Chocolate Chip Lace Cookies, 92
    Chocolate Chip Mandelbrot (Mandel Bread),
        42–43
    Chocolate Fudge Icing, 119
    Chocolate-Covered Pretzels and
        Strawberries, 135–36
    Coconut Pie, 177
    Cranberry Lace Cookies, 140
    Cream Cheese Frosting, 91
    Dede's Sour Cream Coffee Cake, 142–43
    Delicious Classic Cheesecake with an Oreo
        Cookie Crust, 172–73
    Dottie's Noodle Pudding, 169
    Edith's Orange Cake, 141
    Graham Cracker Crust, 26
    Grandma Leah's Kichala, 54–55
    Honey Cake, 40–42
    Ice Cream Pie, 26–27
    Katie's Lemon Cake, 144–45
    Lemon Icing, 145
    Matzo Brickle for Passover, 148
    New, Old-Fashioned Hamantaschen,
        131–32
    Orange Glaze, 141
    Passover Brownies, 117
    Passover Tart, 149
    Rugelach, 66–67
    Rum Pound Cake, 176
    Super-Rich Fudge Cake, 178–79
    Sweet Potato Pudding, 179
    See also fruit
Dilled Carrots, 22
    dips, dressings and sauces
    about: toppings for latkes, 86
    Avocado-Tomato Dip, 10
    Creamy Vinaigrette Dressing, 89
    Egg and Caviar Spread, 33
    Lemon Sauce, 56
    Spinach Dip, 9
    Sweet Salad Dressing, 116
    Sweet-and-Sour Poppyseed Dressing, 24
    Whitefish Dip, 12
Dottie's Noodle Pudding, 169
dreidel (the game), 93
dressings. *See* dips, dressings and sauces
drinks. *See* specialty drinks; wine

E

Edith's Orange Cake, 141
Edith's Red Wine Brisket, 38–39
Egg and Caviar Spread, 33

equipment, 4

Escalloped Potatoes, 139

everyday, making sacred, 31–32

F

fail-safe crowd-pleasers, 6

fasting

    breaking. *See* breaking the fast

    tips, 51

first-aid tips, 7

fish and seafood

    Crabmeat Appetizer, 47

    Egg and Caviar Spread, 33

    Gefilte Fish, 101

    Tuna Salad with Dill, 60

    Whitefish Dip, 12

5-Cup Fruit Salad (Ambrosia), 59

Flourless Potato Pancakes, 84–85

Fresh String Beans with Garlic Butter, 36

fruit

    about: blessing over, 129; as fail-safe
        crowd-pleaser, 11

    Easy Homemade Pear-Infused
        Applesauce, 87

    5-Cup Fruit Salad (Ambrosia), 59

    Fresh Fruit, 11

    Fruit and Cheese Appetizer, 75

    Raspberry-Cranberry Jell-O Mold, 52–53

    See also specific fruits

G

Gefilte Fish, 101

Grandma Edith's Onion Noodle Kugel, 20

Grandma Rose's Popover Recipe, 175

Greengrass, Rachel, 31–32

guests, preparing for, 3

H

Haggadah, 96, 97, 105–8

Hamantaschen, New, Old-Fashioned,
    131–32

holidays

    essential ingredients to stock, 1–2

    See also specific holidays

Homemade Potato Salad, 64

honey

    about: blessings over apples and, 44

    Honey Cake, 40–42

    Honeyed Chicken Wings, 76

I

Ice Cream Pie, 26–27

ingredients

    essential holiday items, 1–2

    organizing and preparing, 5

    See also specific ingredients

injuries, treating, 7

J

Jewish BBQ Brisket, 154–57

K

Kichala, Grandma Leah's, 54–55

kitchen

    cleaning tips, 5

    essential ingredients to stock, 1–2

injuries in, treating, 7
knowing oven and, 5–6
organizing ingredients, 5
safety, 6, 7
knowing kitchen/oven, 5–6
kosher
    facts about, 62–63
    keeping, 62, 63
    rules, 62–63
    separating meat and dairy, 63
    wine, 25
Kosher Caipirinha, 132–33
kugel
    Apple-Raisin Noodle Kugel, 137
    Grandma Edith's Onion Noodle
        Kugel, 20

L

latkes, 69, 72, 84–86
Leavy, Jane, 45
Lebowitz, Fran, 135
leftovers, 12–13, 89, 109, 115, 118, 160
lemons
    Katie's Lemon Cake, 144–45
    Lemon Icing, 145
    Lemon Sauce, 56
Lewis, Richard, 1
lists
    holiday ingredient essentials, 1–2
    pans, dishes, and equipment, 4

M

Mashed Potatoes, 158

matzo
    about: questions/answers on, 112–13
    Baby David's Chicken Soup with White
        Meatballs (Matzo Balls), 102
    Matzo Balls (White Meatballs), 103
    Matzo Bread Crumbs, 12
    Matzo Brei, 121
    Matzo Brickle for Passover, 148
Meir, Golda, 95
menorah, lighting, 72
menu-planning tips, 2
metric conversions, 180
Mimi Chicken, 164–65
Mozzarella and Tomato Salad, 49

N

New, Old-Fashioned Hamantaschen, 131–32
noodles
    Apple-Raisin Noodle Kugel, 137
    Aunt Judy's Sweet Noodle Pudding, 37
    Chicken Noodle Soup, 48
    Dottie's Noodle Pudding, 169
    Grandma Edith's Onion Noodle Kugel, 20

O

Onion Noodle Kugel, Grandma Edith's, 20
oven, knowing, 5–6

P

pans, dishes, and equipment, 4
pantry/refrigerator, holiday essentials, 1–2
Passover, 95–125
    about: creative approach to, 32; facts

about, 96–97, 101; Four Questions, 101, 125; Haggadah, 96, 97, 105–8; matzo balls, 112–13; overview of, 95; real world traditions, 98–99; seder songs, 122–25; wine suggestions, 95

Almond Macaroons, 120

Aunt Frieda's Nut Cake, 118–19

Baby David's Chicken Soup with White Meatballs (Matzo Balls), 102

Broccoli Soufflé, 109

Charoset, 104

Chopped Liver, 100

Gefilte Fish, 101

Matzo Balls (White Meatballs), 103

Matzo Brei, 121

Matzo Brickle for Passover, 148

Passover Brownies, 117

Passover Rolls, 114

Passover Tart, 149

Red Potatoes, 115

Roast Turkey, 110–11

Sweet Salad Dressing, 116

Pear-Infused Applesauce, Easy Homemade, 87

Pink Ginger Skyy Martini, 73

Popover Recipe, Grandma Rose's, 175

Poppyseed Dressing, Sweet-and-Sour, 24

Pot Roast, 161

potatoes
Escalloped Potatoes, 139
Flourless Potato Pancakes, 84–85
Homemade Potato Salad, 64
Mashed Potatoes, 158

Potato Varenikas, 162–63
Red Potatoes, 115

prayer, kinds of, 32

preparation
for guests, 3
importance of, 5

Pretzels, Chocolate-Covered, 135–36

Purim
about, 130
Kosher Caipirinha, 132–33
New, Old-Fashioned Hamantaschen, 131–32

R

Raspberry-Cranberry Jell-O Mold, 52–53

real world traditions
Chanukah, 70–71
Passover, 98–99
Rosh Hashanah, 35
Shabbat, 16–17

Red Potatoes, 115

Roast Turkey, 110–11

Rosh Hashanah, 29–44
about: blessings, 44; facts about, 30; making the everyday sacred and, 31–32; message from rabbi Rachel Greengrass, 31–32; overview of, 29; real world traditions, 35; sounds of shofar, 37; wine suggestions, 29
Aunt Judy's Sweet Noodle Pudding, 37
Chocolate Chip Mandelbrot (Mandel Bread), 42–43
Edith's Red Wine Brisket, 38–39
Egg and Caviar Spread, 33
Fresh String Beans with Garlic Butter, 36

Honey Cake, 40–42
Vegetable Soup, 34–35
Rugelach, 66–67
Rum Pound Cake, 176

S

sacredness, of everyday, 31–32
safety
    tips, 6, 7
salads
    about: dressings for. *See* dips, dressings
        and sauces
    Coleslaw, 65
    Cucumber Salad, 68
    Homemade Potato Salad, 64
    Mozzarella and Tomato Salad, 49
    Raspberry-Cranberry Jell-O Mold, 52–53
    Tuna Salad with Dill, 60
Sandler, Adam, 69
Sangria. *See* specialty drinks
Sarah's Challah French Toast Casserole, 61
sauces. *See* dips, dressings and sauces
Sautéed Broccoli or Cauliflower, 160
Shabbat, 15–28
    about: facts about, 18; forbidden acts on, 21;
        making the everyday sacred and, 31–32;
        overview of, 15; real world traditions,
        16–17; simple blessings for, 28; wine
        suggestions, 15
    Allan's Favorite Garlic Chicken, 22–23
    Dilled Carrots, 22
    Grandma Edith's Onion Noodle Kugel, 20
    Ice Cream Pie, 26–27

Spinach Cheese Squares, 19
Sweet-and-Sour Poppyseed Dressing, 24
Shofar, sounds of, 37
Simchat Torah, 127–29
songs
    Chanukah, 77–79, 93–94
    Passover seder, 122–25
soups and stews
    Baby David's Chicken Soup with White
        Meatballs (Matzo Balls), 102
    Cabbage Borscht, 168
    Chicken Noodle Soup, 48
    Chicken Stew, 13
specialty drinks
    about, 73
    Kosher Caipirinha, 132–33
    Pink Ginger Skyy Martini, 73
    Red Sangria, 74
    White Sangria, 74
spinach
    Spinach Cheese Squares, 19
    Spinach Dip, 9
strawberries
    Chocolate Covered Strawberries, 135–36
    Fresh Fruit, 11
string beans
    Fresh String Beans with Garlic
        Butter, 36
    Vegetable Soup, 34–35
Stuffed Cabbage, 166–67
Stuffed Flank Steak, 50–51
Stuffed Tomatoes, 159
Sukkot, 127–28

Super-Rich Fudge Cake, 178–79
Sweet Potato Pudding, 179
Sweet-and-Sour Poppyseed Dressing, 24

T

take-along foods, 135–51
   Apple Crisp, 150–51
   Apple-Raisin Noodle Kugel, 137
   Blonde Brownies, 146
   Carrot Tzimmis, 138
   Chocolate Chip Banana Bread, 147
   Chocolate-Covered Pretzels and
      Strawberries, 135–36
   Cranberry Lace Cookies, 140
   Dede's Sour Cream Coffee Cake, 142–43
   Edith's Orange Cake, 141
   Escalloped Potatoes, 139
   Katie's Lemon Cake, 144–45
   Matzo Brickle for Passover, 148
   Passover Tart, 149
Talmud quote, 15
tomatoes
   Avocado-Tomato Dip, 10
   Mozzarella and Tomato Salad, 49
   Stuffed Tomatoes, 159
   Vegetable Soup, 34–35
Tu B'Shevat, 129
Turkey, Roast, 110–11

V

vegetables
   about: fail-safe crowd-pleaser, 6
   Roasted Vegetables, 88

Vegetable Basket, 8–9
Vegetable Soup, 34–35
   See also specific vegetables

W

Whitefish Dip, 12
wine
   blessings over, 28, 44
   breaking the fast suggestions, 57
   Chanukah suggestions, 69
   comfort food suggestions, 165, 167
   Edith's Red Wine Brisket, 38–39
   kosher, questions and answers, 25
   kosher, suggestions, 25
   Passover suggestions, 95
   Rosh Hashanah suggestions, 29
   Shabbat suggestions, 15
   Yom Kippur suggestions, 45
   See also specialty drinks

Y

Yom Kippur, 45–56
   about: facts about, 46; fasting tips, 51;
      overview of, 45; wine suggestions, 45
   Asparagus with Lemon Sauce, 56
   Chicken Noodle Soup, 48
   Crabmeat Appetizer, 47
   Grandma Leah's Kichala, 54–55
   Mozzarella and Tomato Salad, 49
   Raspberry-Cranberry Jell-O Mold, 52–53
   Stuffed Flank Steak, 50–51
Youngman, Henny, 29

ABOUT THE AUTHORS

Andrea Marks Carneiro is a freelance writer and editor based in Miami, Florida. She has worked on-staff at several national and regional magazines (including *TALK* and *SouthFloridaCEO*) and has contributed to national and regional media including WE! Television, *Modern Bride,* JuliB.com, and Daily Candy. An amateur at holiday cooking, she is currently honing her skills by practicing on her husband and daughter.

Roz Marks is the go-to gal for all things culinary among her friends and her daughter's friends. A former elementary school teacher, Roz parlayed her people skills and talent for marketing into a twenty-year real estate career. Roz comes from a long line of style-savvy Jewish cooks and spent years learning the traditions of old-world cooking and baking, observing and helping her mother and grandmother, both of whom emigrated from Russia in the early 1900s. She resides in Miami, Florida, with her husband and three rescue dogs.